PARWANA

This book pays homage to the peals of laughter, the tears of loss, the staunch pledges and sacrifices, the lost potential, the ethereal memories and, above all, the dreams of the people of Afghanistan. Of all those who have gone before, and all those still to come.

PARWANA

RECIPES AND STORIES FROM AN AFGHAN KITCHEN

DURKHANAI AYUBI

RECIPES BY FARIDA AYUBI,
WITH ASSISTANCE FROM
FATEMA AYUBI

Interlink Books

An imprint of Interlink Publishing Group, Inc.
Northampton, Massachusetts

Contents

Prelude 9

Chapter 1 Before Parwana 11

Chapter 2 Roots & Belonging 57

Chapter 3 The Dissipation of a Dream 99

Chapter 4 The Plight of the Displaced 161

Chapter 5 The Movable Feast of Culture 203

After Us 245

Acknowledgments 249

About the Author 251

Index 252

PRELUDE

"What you seek is seeking you"

Rumi, thirteenth-century Persian poet and theologian

My family never had any grand plan to be in the restaurant game. Parwana began with my mother Farida (pictured left) and her intuition that, as migrants, it was increasingly important that we preserve the customs, flavors and essence of our Afghan cuisine, and also share it with those in our new home. She carried with her a generationally engrained love for her traditional food and the rituals that sit alongside it. This, combined with our experience as displaced people, witnessing first-hand the scattering effects of war on Afghanistan's memory and culture, coaxed Parwana into being. In this way, Parwana was driven by commemoration, reconciliation, and creativity, tinged with a mixture of loss and hope.

However, in hindsight, the strands of the idea had long existed in many guises, and had been finding their way to us to consolidate and express, well before we opened the doors to Parwana in 2009. The restaurant, and the food we shared, was a manifestation of the immense history of cross-pollination and cultural exchange that underpinned Afghanistan's history at the center of the ancient Silk Road. As time marched on and change unfolded on the land, including the emergence of Afghanistan as a nation state, this was captured in the cuisine and the traditions surrounding it. By the time the heavy clouds of conflict gathered overhead, my family had migrated to Australia—and, with the emotions of exile, whose challenges and opportunities were now ours to carry, food took on a new poignancy and significance. Food was never static, but an ever-evolving way to stay anchored to our history while filling our sails with hopes for tomorrow. For us, food had become a means to tell a bigger story. This book contains not only recipes, but also the history and energies that lie behind them.

An awareness of these histories and energies is important, even necessary, for understanding Afghan cuisine in a way that extends beyond the superficial. For too long the dominant narrative surrounding Afghanistan has been trapped in the idea of its conquest, taming and manipulation by those who seek to control it. Images of violence and catastrophe

almost always prevail. The inference in all these images is one of a nation far too hostile and foreign, too "other," to engage with, or a wasteland to be pitied. And, although it is true that many Afghan people have suffered over generations, the reasons for this suffering are intimately linked to prevailing narratives that consign and reduce the region, and the people in it, to a position that is distant and irreconcilable.

But the truths about Afghanistan that are becoming increasingly pertinent to understand, against the globally intertwined reality of our world today, are the stories of the interconnection that underpins it. The way in which this interconnection has been captured in the food, ingredients, flavors, rituals, and experiences of my family, I hope to unfold in the pages of this book. Furthermore, in Afghan custom, where historical ties run deep and form the lens through which the world is first understood, the stories of food and culture have been threaded together, wherever possible and relevant, by the genealogy of my mother, whose quiet resolution and love for cooking ultimately brought Parwana to life.

Parwana, and the cuisine it shares, hold many layers of significance for us. Both tell a story of the unexpected—as those who dine on Afghan food for the first time find themselves surprised by the familiarity of the dishes, hinting at a rich and interconnected history untold. They tell the story of my mother, who lost her own mother at the age of four and was raised by a father who encouraged her to pursue her love of cooking from a young age. They tell the story of an irrefutable need to ritualize through food, of the permanent and deeply carved imprints of memories otherwise transient and fleeting. They tell the story of who we have come to be, sculpted into shape by the emotional and cultural evolutions we remained attuned to. And, importantly, they tell the story of how we experience firsthand, through food and Parwana, a universal desire to connect, irrespective of perceived differences— hinting at a vision of a future into which we can all move forward together.

Chapter 1

Before
Parwana

فصل اول

THE CROSS-POLLINATION UNDERPINNING CIVILIZATION

فصل اول

"Your spirit is mingled with mine
as wine is mixed with water;
whatever touches you touches me.
In all the stations of the soul you are I."

Al-Hallaj, tenth-century Persian poet and Sufi

My family story, and that of Parwana and the food we share, is the product of millennia of globally significant history that precedes us. In our world today the imagination of many is held captive by the firmly engrained idea of an irreconcilable schism between East and West, but somewhere beyond this reduced narrative lies a rich and intertwined history.

It is a history scarred by the tragic human tendency to inflict suffering in the quest for control; however, importantly, it is also a history shaped by the human capacity for cooperation across seemingly disparate cultures. It is a history of mutual dependence across continents, in the trade of goods and ideas, and the shaping of philosophies. It is a history that, when acknowledged, blurs the boundaries now so firmly, and detrimentally, erected around us. It is a history that points to the commonality of human aspiration, revealing the inseparability of our fates.

Historically and geographically positioned as a witness to the ebb and flow of shared cultural evolution, Afghanistan serves as an icon of this cross-pollination, now largely forgotten, that underpins the human story.

The meeting place of empires

Afghanistan, for its impenetrability and for the failed attempts at its conquest by many foreign powers, has long been known as the "graveyard of empires." In relatively recent history alone, the losses of the British and Russian empires in Afghanistan, as well as the more contemporary, drawn out and hefty occupation by the United States, all reinforce its image as an unconquerable land. But our persistence in seeing Afghanistan predominantly through the lens of war—irrespective of whether we are in awe of its resistance or affronted by its otherness and hostility—limits our vision to a blinkered slither of uncontextualized history.

The region today known as Afghanistan was a landscape in which many great civilizations met and metamorphosed through cultural integration. This was the meeting place of empires; as cultures melded together and evolved in proximity, Afghanistan gave birth to the new.

Afghanistan was host to numerous great empires that rose and fell on its lands—Achaemenid Persians, the Greeks of Alexander the Great, Mauryans of India, Turkic tribes, and the Mongols of Genghis Khan, to name a few. Its ancient cities, such as Bactra, Herat, and later Kabul, grew rich on the thriving trade of its natural resources and became increasingly sophisticated through scholarly advancements; they were beacons of wonder in the ancient world and a flame that drew in poets, artisans, and mystics. The land was home to spectacular gardens laid out by kings, its fertile valleys studded with fruit orchards and rich in natural resources. This was a spiritual heartland—the birthplace of Zoroastrianism, home to the ancient and uninterrupted paganism of Nuristan, an epicenter of Buddhism, Islam, and its mystical expression through Sufism.

For most of its history Afghanistan was not a single country, but a bricolage of unlikely races and cultures, each with its own gods, languages, and customs. While part of the ancient Persian Empire, about 500 BC, its lands were divided into various regions called "satrapies," each with its own governor or "satrap." As parts were consolidated into the Greek Empire, it had been sectioned into a series of provinces, recorded by the Greek historian Herodotus in 440 BC as Bactria, Aria, Parapamisadai, and Arachosia, which roughly mirror the lands of modern Afghanistan. The first iteration of Afghanistan as a consolidated empire emerged in the eighteenth century and existed only fleetingly, under the rule of Ahmad Shah Durrani, known as the "father of Afghanistan." The present-day shape of Afghanistan was traced by the outline of the imperial battles played out between Russia and Britain during the "Great Game" of the nineteenth century, with its own traditional tribal heartlands spilling over the border into what would, in 1947, become Pakistan, following the partition of British India.

East to West and back again: the Silk Road

In much the same way that these firm national boundaries can define simplistic identities, the dominant narratives they have created confine our imagination. Today, it is difficult for many of us to imagine lands in the East as important markers in the trajectory of the human story. Our realities have long been cast in a history in which Rome is the progenitor of Western society, and the dawn of Europe, attributed to Spanish and Portuguese maritime expeditions of the fifteenth century, dominates our vision. In such a history, countries of the East are viewed either as peripheral to the progression of humanity, or as bastions of violence and depravity that have detracted from that progression.

But, thousands of years before the center of the world and control of the stories of our collective past were recast to the West, the early struggles of human culture and civilization began in the fertile lands between the Tigris and Euphrates rivers, in what is present-day Iraq. Rather than Western culture being created in a vacuum, Rome looked to, and was shaped by, the East. The point at which Rome became an empire was in its capture of the fertile, resource-rich, and highly taxable lands of Egypt. Later, the relevance of Rome was maintained by the move of its capital to the East, with the creation of Constantinople where Europe meets Asia. Rather than a narrative of domination of one culture over another, perhaps the human story is better defined as a great exchange— at times in violence and conflict, but also in admiration and the adoption of ideas and philosophies.

Pivotal to this human story of cultural amalgamation and evolution was the pushing of frontiers by China. In the first century BC China extended its reach past the fearsome nomadic tribes to its west and, with this,

My father, Zelmai Ayubi

 قای ایوبی

opened the door into a new world. The Silk Road was born, connecting East with West in both directions. The Silk Road was a series of paths and trading posts—a web of connections rather than a tangible road—that spanned from China to the eastern frontiers of Rome, while other paths cut north from India through the heart of Afghanistan to the Siberian steppes. China traded in prized silks, fine textiles, and other luxury items and, in return, received precious metals, coins, glass, and semi-precious stones. Goods traded hands from post to post; merchant caravans picked up silks and textiles in China, ivories and spices in India, horses from the nomadic tribes of the steppes, precious and semi-precious stones, gold, and tin from Afghanistan, and coins, glass, and metals from Rome. Importantly, it was not just merchants and goods that traversed the route. Warriors, conquerors, pilgrims,

tenet of this global story. When Silk Road trade and transit first began to thrive, Afghanistan was part of the Kushan Empire of the Yuezhi, an ancient nomadic people of Indo-European origin. The Kushan Empire adapted many of the Hellenistic traditions of the lands they subsumed, and ruled over a region that includes today's Afghanistan and surrounding areas. Historians place the empire's summer capital at Begram in Afghanistan. In the 1930s two sealed-off rooms were unearthed in Begram; they contained a trove of ancient artifacts, including plaster medallions, bronzes, and painted glassware from Rome, lacquered porcelains from China, and carved ivories from India. That these were all found in a single location, in a significant city of an ancient Indo-Afghan dynasty with deep Hellenistic roots, reveals a highly connected world of old. But, more than that, the artifacts

nomads, and artists coursed along the pathways like blood through veins, spreading the ideas and customs that shaped the trajectory of the human story. The highly linked world of antiquity, much like our present world, was challenged by globalization while wanting to be vibrant and competitive and spurred to progress through innovation.

The Silk Road existed long before maritime routes could facilitate trade between continents. Its glory days were the centuries following the first millennium, and it remained in heavy use until the fifteenth century. Situated at the geographical heart of the thriving, bustling Silk Road, Afghanistan was a central

depicted scenes of Buddhist, Hellenistic and Roman gods and a marbling of artistic styles, reflecting Roman-Egyptian, Graeco-Egyptian, Indo-Iranian and Graeco-Indian fusions. It revealed a world in which dissimilar cultures not only cohabited, but cross-referenced and were shaped by one another.

Lands of ancient globalization

But the story of Afghanistan begins long before the defining centuries of the Silk Road. Archaeological digs have revealed the region to be home to some of the earliest modern humans, with tools unearthed that date back tens of thousands of years to the Paleolithic Age or earlier. The indigenous people of Afghanistan (estimated by anthropologist Louis Dupree to have populated the land from at least 50,000 BC) were likely small herders and farmers who existed in tribes. Their exact origin has been washed away with the tide of time, but they developed some of the earliest farming communities. As early as 7000 BC farmers and herders settled in the foothills of the Hindu Kush, making it one of the first places on earth where animals and plants were domesticated.

Such sites are thought to have grown wealthy from an abundance of lapis lazuli and tin, which, long before the advent of the Silk Road, were most likely traded with other early civilizations in Iran and Mesopotamia to the west. Increasingly sophisticated irrigation systems were developed, allowing the desert plains to become fertile and, in conjunction with this agricultural evolution, complex rituals and craftsmanship developed, leading to a thriving Bronze Age in the region. A set of golden bowls chanced upon by farmers in Teppe Fullol, in the north of Afghanistan, and dated to 4000 years ago, reveal fusions of artwork mixing local elements with styles from distant cultures of the Middle East. Such finds show that, as early as the Bronze Age, the people of Afghanistan were involved in international trade.

It was not only early material developments that took place in Afghanistan, but spiritual milestones too. According to the ancient Zoroastrian text Avesta, Bactra (modern-day Balkh in the north of Afghanistan) is the birthplace of Zoroaster, making Afghanistan the spiritual homeland of the world's earliest monotheistic faith. With its concepts of a single god and the dualism of good and evil, Zoroastrianism is regarded as a precursor to the world's major faiths, and remains one of the oldest continuously practiced religions. To this day, the New Year festivals in Afghanistan and Iran, known as Nowruz ("new day"), are embedded in the Zoroastrian tradition of celebrating the spring equinox. Zoroastrianism was the primary faith of Cyrus the Great's Achaemenid Empire in the sixth century BC, and Bactra the main stronghold of this dynasty.

Before long, the gaze of Alexander the Great fell on these lands, and in 329 BC Alexander and his 40,000-strong army swept through the region, leaving behind a trail of cities bearing his name, and thousands of newly arrived Greeks to live in them. It was in Bactra, the furthest Hellenistic reach from the Greek homeland, that Alexander is said to have married Roxanne, the daughter of a Bactrian leader. After Alexander's death in 323 BC, the Hellenistic

presence persisted throughout Afghanistan, first under the rule of one of Alexander's former commanders, Seleucus, and then for centuries with the emergence of a distinct Graeco-Bactrian dynasty.

Iconic of this culture, an entire Greek city, complete with palace, gymnasium, temple, and theater, was excavated in the 1960s, just west of Bactra at Ai Khanum. Despite its many Hellenic hallmarks, including inscriptions in the Greek language, the city had been adapted to reflect local architectural influences and Eastern-style ground plans. The discovery provides tangible evidence of the foreign influences, themselves in turn influenced by local customs, which would become a persistent part of local culture.

Greek influence on the local culture was not exclusive. In the third century BC, Seleucus attempted to expand his empire to include India, an evasive jewel in the eye of many from the West, but he was repelled by Chandragupta Maurya, the figurehead of India's great Mauryan Empire. As part of a peace treaty, Seleucus conceded a portion of his empire in Afghanistan to the Mauryans. Under the rule of Chandragupta's grandson, Ashoka the Great, Buddhism streamed into the Afghan consciousness. Ashoka, a convert to Buddhism, was an ardent patron and pioneer of its message. Buddhist stupas were built throughout Afghanistan and, during Ashoka's reign from 269–232 BC, Buddhism spread from Afghanistan eastwards into China and westwards to the Mediterranean. Afghanistan had now become a spiritual heartland for Zoroastrianism, a pantheon of Greek gods and an array of Buddhist deities.

After Ashoka's death the Mauryan Empire gradually crumbled, and the power vacuum this created was filled by the Kushans. Once nomadic, the Kushans settled in Bactra and surrounds and adopted the most appealing customs of those they had dispossessed. The result was a vibrant new culture, fusing together Graeco-Bactrian ideals and Eastern traditions, administered through the lens of the Kushans' traits and personalities. Coins were minted, featuring Greek language alongside the faces of Kushan royalty, and Buddhism was reinforced and spread through the efforts of Kanishka, the third king of this dynasty. Positioned at the center of the Silk Road, at a time when trade across the world was thriving, the Kushans became one of the wealthiest and most powerful dynasties of this era, second only to the might of China and Rome.

This potpourri of influences was expressed in the artwork of the region and exemplified in the unlikely fusions found in cross-cultural artifacts, such as the Aphrodite of Bactria found at a site at Tillya Tepe and dated to the first century AD. The artifact, a small golden ornament, is the Greek goddess Aphrodite, but with the wings of a Bactrian deity and the forehead marking of Indian tradition. This is but one symbol of an era of peaceful coexistence under Kushan rule: religious tolerance was exemplified by the coins bearing a panoply of cross-cultural deities that were in wide circulation and by the proliferation of different temples, as Zoroastrian, Buddhist, Hindu, Jewish, and the newly emerged Christian communities lived side by side.

The evolution of empires, from the Mongol hordes to the Mughals

Sitting at the center of East and West also had its downfalls: the land was sensitive to the rise and fall of neighboring empires. The crumbling of China's Han Dynasty and the near collapse of the Roman Empire in the third century simultaneously diminished the prosperity of Silk Road trade and contributed to the demise of the Kushan Empire. The region fell to the Sassanian Empire, one of the last great kingdoms of Persia before the cataclysmic rise of Islam in the seventh century—the force that revolutionized Afghanistan once more. The newly coalesced Arabs spread Islam in Afghanistan via the towns of Kandahar and Ghazni. The Islamic empires that rose and fell in Afghanistan during the period spanning the ninth to the thirteenth centuries included the Saffarids, the Ghaznavids, and the Ghurids. Notably, it was not until the time of the Ghaznavids, whose founder was a Turkish slave, that large parts of Afghanistan, including Kabul, were united under consolidated rule. It was also during the era of the Ghurids in 1207 that Jalaloddin Balkhi—Rumi—was born, either in Balkh or nearby Vakhsh. Rumi's verses, dedicated to otherworldly love and entrenched in a deep mysticism derived from Sufism, endure as one of the most widely celebrated bodies of Eastern poetry in the world.

By 1216 Rumi's family had fled Balkh and Samarqand—the towns of his childhood—and migrated west to Anatolia in Turkey. They had felt the impending winds of change that were gathering cyclonic force, in the form of the Mongol hordes of Genghis Khan. The Great Khan and his men thundered across Asia and eventually across continents, razing cities to the ground, claiming territories, and creating the largest land empire ever built. The Mongols became masters of the steppes; they conquered Zhongdu—present day Beijing—in China, spread through Russia, seized the Muslim world in the Middle East, and appeared in parts of Europe. In this quest for global domination, Afghanistan was not spared; Genghis Khan, with an army of 100,000, crossed the Oxus River to conquer Balkh in 1220, snuffing out other beacons of antiquity such as Kabul, Herat, and Bamiyan along the way. The devastation that followed was immense and Balkh—birthplace of Zoroaster, witness of the marriage of Alexander to Roxanne, and crowning jewel of the Silk Road—never fully recovered.

Behind the unparalleled success of the Mongols lay not only their supremacy as warriors, but also their genius as administrators and careful strategists. Alongside the destruction came a recasting of culture, with an enduring imprint left on all those touched by the Mongol might. Culinary habits in China had been altered to reflect the diet of the nomad overlords; language in Russia evolved to incorporate Mongol words; even the fashion sense of European nobility of the Middle Ages had been designed to emulate the conical-shaped headgear of Mongol warriors. The East set the cultural norms. The dynasty of the Great Khans reigned supreme in Afghanistan and their conquered lands for 100 years, until, like most great empires, having spread itself too thin and splintered into sub-branches, it became a victim of its own success and began to crumble.

But there was one legacy of the Mongol Empire that was to influence Afghanistan for centuries to come: the establishment of the Timurid era, whose founder, Timur, was born of Muslim faith and to a Turko-Mongol tribe. Timur was not born into particularly auspicious circumstances, but rose to greatness through ambition and strategic prowess. From the 1360s onwards he built an empire that stretched through Mongol lands from Turkey to China and from Russia to the Persian Gulf. Along the way, he established himself as sovereign of Balkh, with Herat also closely associated with the Timurid name. His empire made for a formidable force, wreaking death and destruction as it marched. However, alongside the carnage, there was an emphasis on creation. Artisans from conquered lands had their lives spared and were, instead, rounded up to create the monuments, gardens, and jewel-studded palaces that bore witness to the empire's reach. Timur's courts at Samarqand were decorated with golden trees, adorned with "fruits" made of rubies, emeralds, turquoise, sapphires, and pearls. As Peter Frankopan describes in *The Silk Roads*,

caravans of up to 800 camels were laden with merchandise from the lands of his subjects, and delivered spices, musk, rubies, and diamonds.

Timur died in the winter of 1405, on his way to conquer China, and Herat was inherited by his son, Shah Rukh. The new ruler focused on nurturing greatness through creativity, rather than bloodletting, and the city reached a cultural zenith; Herat thrived with poets, artists, intellects, and craftsmen who fused together Central Asian and Persian culture, creating architecture, poetry, literature, and scientific advances without rival in Asia. During this era the famous Persian miniature style of art flourished, astronomical observations were used to create charts of the stars (published in Oxford 150 years later), and Sufi luminaries guided decision-making in the royal courts. Missions and embassies from Egypt to China traversed Herat, trading in pure-bred horses, wild animals, and other royal keepsakes. But, as the ruling class became softened by luxuries and complacent in its duties, following the same peaks and troughs

that underpin the trajectory of all great empires, at the opening of the sixteenth century, the flame of the Timurid Empire flickered and dimmed. In 1506, with little resistance, Herat was lost to the Uzbeks, and then within three short years it fell to the Persian Safavids, both of whom should have been no match for the once mighty Timurid Empire.

Crystallized by this pitiful demise, yet of auspicious lineage, was Babur. Descended from Genghis Khan on his mother's side and Timur on his father's, Babur was born in 1483 in the Fergana Valley, where his father was a king. When the valley was invaded by Uzbek tribes, twelve-year-old Babur, a prince by birth, was deprived of the ancestral lands that were to be his inheritance. In his twenties, Babur sought refuge with Timurid relatives in Herat, where he watched as the Timurid Empire took its last breaths in the same manner that his father's lands had been lost. Impoverished, but spurred by the shame of living landless and experiencing firsthand the disintegration of the shining empires of his forebears, Babur rallied some loyal followers. In 1505, at the age of 22, he took Kabul (which came to be his most enduring prize) and later Delhi. This was the beginning of the Mughal Dynasty—which included that long sought-after gem, India—and Babur was its figurehead, followed by his son Humayun and grandson Akbar I.

In a series of personal writings—the first truly autobiographic account of Islamic literature—collated to form the Baburnama ("book of Babur"), Babur emerges as someone with a deep love for nature, and a personality scornful of excess. According to legend, when his son Humayun handed him the Koh-i-Noor diamond—then the largest in the world—he handed it back. (The diamond, with its remarkable history, was later looted by the Persians from the Mughals, then made its way to the Afghans, from where it was passed on to a Sikh child king, Maharaja Duleep Singh, from whom it was appropriated in 1849 by Britain, where it is kept to this day and has adorned the crowns of three British queens.) In other parts of the Baburnama, he accounts for the 33 types of wild tulip that grow on the hillsides of Kabul, and compares the taste of different pomegranate varieties.

In Kabul, Babur built spectacular gardens such as the Bagh-i Wafa, the "garden of fidelity," studded with fountains, pomegranate trees, clover meadows, orange groves, and plants from across his empire. In the Baburnama he describes the Bagh-i Wafa with fondness: "The garden lies high, running water close at hand, and a mild winter climate … In the south-west part there is a reservoir, around which are orange trees and a few pomegranates, the whole enriched by a trefoil meadow. This is the best part of the garden, a most beautiful sight when the oranges take color. Truly, the garden is admirably situated." The emperor and his entourage would picnic in the gardens; cushions would be laid out and tents erected, wine would be drunk, poetry recited, and Sufi music played to the beat of traditional tambours. Babur lived an extraordinary life, beginning in misfortune and ending as an emperor of swathes of land. His final wish was to be buried in Kabul, among his beloved gardens. Babur died in Agra in 1530, after being struck by fever, and by 1544 his body had been moved and laid to rest in the Bagh-e Babur, one of the ten gardens he designed and cultivated in Afghanistan.

Although Mughal rule in Afghanistan survived until the British took control of the government in the nineteenth century, in actuality, by the fifteenth and sixteenth centuries, the sun was beginning to set on Herat, and ultimately all of Central Asia. The shadow of decline was cast by a confluence of factors: the superiority of the weapons of the empires that had begun to surround it; the opening of maritime routes by the Spanish and Portuguese, offering cheaper and faster trading alternatives to the previously unchallenged monopoly of the Silk Road land routes; and the rise in power and prevalence of a once distant and obscure land, Russia.

History on the menu

It is from this long and intertwined history that the cuisine of Afghanistan and the culture surrounding it emerged. Alongside the emperors, religions, and artifacts that crisscrossed the Silk Road into Afghanistan came a panoply of impressive culinary offerings from across the globe. From India came the variety of dahls and the prized spices, so intensely sought after throughout the West, including chilies, turmeric, saffron, cumin, cinnamon, cloves, nutmeg, and pepper. These spices, apportioned in delicate amounts, became a mainstay of Afghan cooking—seared daily into meats and curries, and baked into rice dishes and vegetables. Special mixes of four different spices, named chaar masalah and often unique to each household, form the flavor base of sauces and palaws, giving rise to the gentle and fragrant aromas typical of Afghan cooking. From the ancient shared history with Persia came the cilantro, mint, and other green herbs that are now so prevalent in Afghan cuisine. From China and Mongolia came a tradition of hand-rolled noodles, known as aush, and dumplings, adapted to reflect the milder Afghan palate and stuffed with natively grown vegetables such as gandana. From Turkey and the Middle East came the sweet floral notes of rose water and syrup-drenched nutty desserts.

And from the lands of Afghanistan itself—a region home to some of the earliest known examples of domestication of livestock and irrigation to create arable pasture—comes the liberal use of dairy and a diet inclusive of meat such as goat, beef, and lamb. The country has a widely varied topography, creating the right conditions for a plethora of crops to thrive. Its warmer plains have the conditions conducive for wheat, corn, rice, and barley—all staples that form the basis of the Afghan diet; these are milled and baked into hot naans or used to create the rice dishes that form the centerpiece of Afghan dining. Other areas sit high above sea level in fertile valleys at the base of the mountain ranges, where the pure mountain waters that gush down in winter and spring are redirected as needed to cultivate fruit and nut orchards. Afghanistan grows pistachios, almonds, pine nuts, grapes, melons, plums, apricots, cherries, figs, mulberries, and pomegranates. These have long been enjoyed fresh, or dried as snacks to serve with tea, and have been worked assiduously into the cuisine; they adorn rice dishes like jewels or are infused into sauces and curries, adding base notes of flavor and an undeniable element of beauty and artistry.

Inseparable from Afghan food is the style that encapsulates it. The way in which food is enjoyed reflects the gregarious spirit that underpins the ritual of eating in Afghan custom. Food is rarely served as individual portions, but piled copiously onto large platters from which everyone helps themselves. And a meal rarely consists of a single dish—but an array of dishes spread out, from which smaller portions all placed together on a plate make a full meal. Alongside main dishes, such as rices, curries, meats, or dumplings, sits an assortment of accompaniments—pickles, preserves, chutneys, fresh vegetables, hot naans, or yogurts—to add bursts of acidic citrus flavor, freshness, and texture. This feeling of generosity often begins long before and continues long after the meal is served. Food is hardly ever prepared in isolation, more usually with others. And the highest tenet of eating in Afghanistan, perhaps its holy grail, is the hospitality that surrounds it. Unexpected guests are treated with the utmost care and attention; even those who have very little to share will ensure their guests are always treated to the best.

Aside from the offering of food, the belief in hospitality is embedded in a spirit of servitude—the place of the guest in a home is equated to near-divinity, and the role of the host is to ensure the visitor leaves with a sense of dignity perhaps even greater than when they arrived. Given the long history of Afghanistan at the heart of the Silk Road—a place where many guests proclaimed themselves messengers of divinity, or were merchants and traders with riches to share—it is easy to see why the custom of hospitality has become so deeply engrained in the genetics of Afghans.

Just like the forging together of many cultures in Afghanistan, the intermingling of local and introduced ingredients and the arising customs surrounding food have created a cuisine that is simultaneously familiar and unique. Such culinary transmutation is an act of creativity analogous to our constant human evolution, making Afghan cuisine emblematic of a story into which we have all been written.

The recipes in this chapter have been chosen for their reflection of the shared ancient history that has given rise to Afghan cuisine, and of the congenial spirit that underlies the culture of food in the region.

THE RITUAL OF NOWROZ

Among the first few recipes in the chapter are some dishes usually prepared to commemorate Nowroz, a New Year celebration that is significant throughout Afghanistan, Iran, and across Central Asia.

The Nowroz festival coincides with the spring equinox in March and, just like the full circle of the seasons, it is symbolic of rebirth. Predating Islam, Nowroz is an ancient celebration that traces its roots to Zoroastrianism, the spiritual homeland of which is said to be Balkh, Afghanistan. The color associated with Nowroz is green, reflecting the Zoroastrian tradition of marking the spring equinox and celebrating the new life it brings.

Afghan communities around the world celebrate Nowroz with general festivities in the lead-up to the day, including the preparation of specific dishes at home, such as haft mewa, sabzi, and kolcheh Nowrozi, which are all included in this chapter. In my parents' youth, it was a time for picnics, sweets, and flying kites. As a child, my mother recalls making an annual trip with her family to Mazar-e Sharif in the north of the country to a festival known as Meleh Gule Sorkh. There, the desert plains would be transformed into fields of red tulips, heralding the start of spring.

CHAAR MASALAH

چار مساله

4 cinnamon sticks
8 dried bay leaves
7 brown cardamom pods
2 tablespoons green cardamom pods
2 tablespoons cumin seeds
2½ tablespoons coriander seeds
2 teaspoons cloves

Chaar masalah translates as "four spices," but rather than literally meaning a blend of four spices, it generally refers to a mix of multiple spices, which can be used as a flavor base for many different dishes. The spices used vary from one region to the next, and even from one household to the next, but usually include a selection of warm spices such as cumin, coriander, cardamom, pepper, cinnamon, turmeric, saffron, and nutmeg.

Chaar masalah is similar in concept to the garam masalah, meaning "hot spices," of Mughal origin that is used extensively in traditional Indian cooking. However, compared to that of some of its South Asian neighbors, Afghan cuisine is milder, and chili is generally added fresh to taste, rather than being used in powdered form in a spice mix.

The chaar masalah recipe given here is the one used in our kitchen at Parwana, and it will be referred to in recipes throughout this book. The choice and proportion of spices in the blend has been fine-tuned over the years to create a delicate balance of warmth, flavor, and fragrance, designed to bring out the best natural qualities of the ingredients to which it is added—but it can of course be adapted to suit your own tastes.

Dry-roast all the ingredients in a nonstick frying pan over low heat for 3 minutes, or until fragrant. Keep a close eye on them and shake the pan frequently so they don't burn. Set aside to cool completely.

Once cooled, transfer to a spice grinder or mortar and pestle, and grind to a fine powder.

Store chaar masalah in a tightly sealed jar, where it will keep for up to 6 months. But note that the potency of the mix corresponds to its freshness, so it's best used within a few weeks of being made.

HAFT MEWA

هفت ميوه

Haft mewa literally translates as "seven fruits" and is a type of compote comprising a selection of dried fruit and nuts, steeped in water until their flavors and natural sweetness emerge and combine. Traditionally, it is made once a year to mark the ritual of Nowroz.

Despite the translation, haft mewa can, and often does, include more than seven different fruits and nuts. Different families use different ingredients because the recipe is flexible enough to vary according to personal preference and taste.

This recipe is one my mother grew up with, and which we continue to make generations later. It includes two types of dried apricots: those widely available in supermarkets, and a specific type of Afghan dried apricot that is dehydrated and a little sour, which can be found in Afghan and Persian grocery shops. Sinjid, also known as dried Russian olives, are also available from Afghan and Persian grocery shops.

Start this recipe two days ahead of serving to allow time for the flavors to develop.

⅔ cup (3½ oz/100 g) whole almonds
1 cup (3½ oz/100 g) walnuts
¾ cup (3½ oz/100 g) pistachios
2 cups (10½ oz/300 g) golden raisins
⅔ cup (3½ oz/100 g) raisins
¾ cup (3½ oz/100 g) whole dried apricots
½ cup (3½ oz/100 g) whole dried sour apricots, with seeds
⅔ cup (3½ oz/100 g) sinjid (dried Russian olives)
12 cups (3 liters) boiling water

Soak each variety of nut separately in bowls of hot water for at least 30 minutes to help with peeling. Once the skins are slightly softened, drain the nuts and use your fingers to rub off the skins, dropping the skinned nuts into a very large heatproof container that has a lid.

Add all the dried fruit to the nuts and mix well, then pour in the boiling water, place the lid on top, and set aside to cool. Refrigerate for 2 days to let the flavors fully develop.

Serve chilled, ladling some syrup into each bowl. Haft mewa will keep refrigerated in an airtight container for up to a week.

SABZI

سبزی چلو

Sabzi is a type of spinach and lamb curry that is traditionally served on Nowroz alongside a rice dish called challaw (see page 111). It is included in the Nowroz spread because of the green color of spinach and its association with the fresh new growth of spring.

At Parwana, we make this dish in a pressure cooker, to help tenderize the lamb. Pressure cookers are often used to help seal in flavor, create a uniform tenderness, and substantially reduce cooking times. If you don't have one, use a heavy-based saucepan or Dutch oven to cook the lamb instead; however, you'll need to add 2 cups (500 ml) more water than the recipe states and the cooking time will increase to about an hour, or until there is approximately 1 cup (250 ml) liquid left.

Note that for vegetarian and vegan diets, sabzi can be made without the lamb, or with kidney beans alongside the spinach instead.

1 cup (250 ml) sunflower oil
1 large yellow onion, finely diced
2 garlic cloves, finely chopped
1 fresh, long red chili, thinly sliced
2¼ lb (1 kg) boneless lamb leg, cut
   into chunks
3 bunches (2¼ lb/1 kg) spinach, washed
   thoroughly, roots and stalks removed
½ cup (125 ml) boiling water
1 small bunch (2¾ oz/ 80 g) cilantro,
   leaves and stalks finely chopped
1 small bunch (2¼ oz/60 g) garlic chives,
   finely chopped
Salt

Pour half the oil into a pressure cooker pan over high heat and fry the onion, garlic, and chili, stirring regularly for 5 minutes, or until golden brown. Add the lamb and sear until it has browned all over. Add 3 cups (750 ml) water and 2 tablespoons salt, then close the lid of the pressure cooker. Bring up to high pressure, then reduce the heat to low and cook for 20 minutes. Remove the cooker from the heat and set aside, allowing the pressure to release naturally.

Meanwhile, finely chop the spinach leaves. Place in a large saucepan with the boiling water, cover the pan with a lid, and cook, stirring occasionally, over medium-high heat for about 20 minutes, or until all the liquid has been absorbed.

Next, heat the remaining oil in a frying pan over medium heat and fry the cilantro and garlic chives, stirring occasionally, for 5 minutes, to bring out the flavors.

Add the lamb to the spinach along with 1 cup (250 ml) of its cooking liquid and the fried herbs. Stir to combine well, then simmer for 15 minutes over low heat for the flavors to mingle.

This sabzi is traditionally enjoyed with a plate of challaw and a dollop of yogurt alongside.

MAASTEH KHANAGI

حاشت خانگی

The Afghan diet includes liberal amounts of yogurt—either spooned onto plates alongside a main meal or whisked together with garlic and salt, and drizzled over savory dishes to balance out other flavors.

This homemade yogurt is rich and frothy, and tastes much earthier than store-bought yogurts. After the initial batch is made, keep a portion aside to use as the starter culture for your next batch.

Afghans also use yogurt to make a special type of dairy product called chaka: the yogurt is wrapped in cheesecloth and hung up to drain for 4–5 hours. Once dried, the yogurt hardens into chaka, which will keep for a week or so, refrigerated. Before serving, it is mixed with a trickle of water until it is thick and creamy again, and seasoned with salt to taste. Chaka has a sharp flavor and distinctive aroma. It can be used in place of yogurt for aush soup (see page 224), and braised vegetable dishes such as banjaan borani (see page 169) and kadoo borani (see page 179).

6 cups (1.5 liters) whole milk
3 dried bay leaves
2 tablespoons plain Greek-style yogurt
  with live and active cultures

Bring the milk and bay leaves to a boil in a small saucepan, then remove the pan from the heat and set aside to cool to 122°F (50°C) or until still hot, but not scorching or lukewarm, to touch.

Whisk the yogurt into the milk until frothy, then pour into a clay pot or other suitable lidded container, such as a glass or stainless-steel bowl. Cover the container with a clean tea towel and place a lid securely on top. Wrap the whole thing in a thick blanket and place it somewhere warm or at room temperature where it won't be moved for 10 hours—it is important that the yogurt is left undisturbed, or it will not set.

After the 10-hour setting period, place the yogurt in the fridge, where it will keep fresh for 2–3 days.

KOLCHEH NOWROZI

کلچه نوروزی

1 cup and 2 tbsp (9 oz/250 g) butter
2½ cups (11 oz/310 g) confectioners'
  sugar, plus 2½ tablespoons to serve
2 large eggs
2½ tablespoons rosewater
3 cups (13 oz/375 g) self-rising flour
2 cups (11¼ oz/320 g) rice flour
Edible wafer paper and finely ground
  pistachios, to serve (optional)
Salt

These cookies are made specifically for Nowroz celebrations. Rarely made at home, they are mostly bought from local Afghan bakeries that specialize in making traditional sweets. During the festivities, small shop windows are piled high with an assortment of sweet treats placed on sheets of colored tissue paper. This recipe uses rice flour to give the cookies a light and airy texture.

◆

Using an electric mixer, cream the butter and sugar until pale and creamy. Add the eggs, one at a time, mixing until thoroughly incorporated before adding the next. Add the rosewater and mix well, then sift in both types of flour and a pinch of salt. Using a wooden spoon, mix until a soft and slightly sticky dough forms.

Turn out the dough onto a lightly floured surface and knead for 2 minutes, or until the dough loses its stickiness. Wrap the dough in plastic wrap and refrigerate for 30 minutes to firm up.

Meanwhile, preheat the oven to 350°F (180°C) and line a large baking pan with parchment paper.

Divide the dough into 12 roughly equal portions and roll by hand into smooth balls. Place them on the pan, spacing them out well, and flatten into 4 in (10 cm) discs. Using a fork, gently press down on the middle of each cookie to create shallow grooves in the top.

Place the pan in the center of the oven and bake the cookies for 15 minutes, or until they are firm and a very pale gold color—they should not be overly browned. Set aside to cool.

Traditionally, these cookies are served on squares of colorful tissue paper. If you want to do the same, substitute the edible wafer paper for tissue paper. Cut your preferred paper into squares slightly larger than the cookies. Add the extra confectioners' sugar to a small bowl and slowly stir in 1–1½ teaspoons cold water, drop by drop, until a thick, milky paste forms. Use this to glue the colored paper squares to the base of the cookies. You can also spread a small coin-sized amount of the paste on top of each cookie and sprinkle with ground pistachios. Kolcheh Nowrozi will keep for up to a week in an airtight container.

MAHEE

ماهی

Heaped 1 tablespoon garlic powder
Heaped 1 tablespoon ground coriander
Heaped 1 tablespoon ground red pepper
  4 small whole fish, such as yellowtail
  kingfish, whiting, or hake, scaled
  and gutted
1¼ cups (5¼ oz/150 g) all-purpose flour
Canola oil for deep-frying
Lemon slices, to serve
Salt

Afghanistan is a landlocked country and, as such, seafood does not feature heavily in its cuisine. However, the rivers teem with freshwater fish, particularly in the winter months leading up to Nowroz. Rainbow trout and brown trout are commonly found in the streams beneath the mountain ranges, and a type of barbel known as shir mahee is found in the waterways of the Hindu Kush.

Traditionally, during Nowroz, shopfronts display trays of small, crunchy deep-fried fish alongside trays of a sticky sweet called jelabi. The significance of the fish for Nowroz is two-fold: it is both seasonal and, as in many cultures and faiths around the world, an auspicious symbol of new life. It is paired with jelabi to add sweetness to any new undertakings.

These spicy fish can be eaten with jelabi (see page 33), as per the Nowroz tradition, or with naan flatbread (see page 82) and raw vegetables such as radish and scallions with a squeeze of lemon juice, or any vegetables of your choice.

Mix the garlic powder, spices, and 1 tablespoon salt in a small bowl to combine, then generously rub both sides of each fish with the mixture.

Scatter the flour over a tray or large plate and coat both sides of the spiced fish with flour, gently shaking off any excess.

In a deep-fryer or large heavy-based saucepan, heat enough oil for deep-frying to about 350°F (180°C) on an oil thermometer, or until large bubbles form around the handle of a wooden spoon placed in the oil—if the bubbles are small, the oil isn't hot enough.

Working in batches of 2 at a time, so as not to overcrowd the pan, gently lower the fish into the oil and fry, turning once, for 4–5 minutes, or until golden brown and crunchy.

Remove with a slotted spoon, drain on paper towels, and keep warm while you cook the rest of the fish. Serve hot, with lemon slices.

JELABI

1¾ cups (5¼ oz/150 g) all-purpose flour
⅔ cup (2½ oz/75 g) self-rising flour
2½ tablespoons plain yogurt
¼ cup (60 ml) lukewarm water
½ teaspoon baking soda
Pinch of citric acid
Sunflower oil for deep-frying

FOR THE SYRUP
3½ cups (1¼ lb/550 g) sugar
½ teaspoon saffron threads
½ teaspoon ground cardamom

Enjoyed during Nowroz alongside mahee fried fish (see page 30), but also made for celebrations, including Eid, or for weddings and engagement parties, jelabi is a deep-fried, syrup-coated sweet. In Afghanistan, it is often sold by street vendors, and is also eaten in neighboring countries, including India and Pakistan.

Sift both types of flour into a bowl. Add the yogurt and warm water, and whisk until you have a smooth, runny batter with a consistency similar to that of pancake batter.

Cover with plastic wrap and set aside at room temperature to rest for 2 hours.

Meanwhile, for the syrup, add the sugar to a small saucepan with 2½ cups (625 ml) water and whisk over low heat until the sugar dissolves. Increase the heat and bring to a boil, then reduce the heat to medium and simmer, without stirring, for 10 minutes. Stir in the saffron and cardamom to combine and set aside to cool.

Once the batter has rested, add the baking soda and citric acid, and mix well. Pour the batter into a squeezy bottle ready to pipe into the hot oil.

In a deep-fryer or large wok, heat enough oil for deep-frying to 350°F (180°C) on an oil thermometer, or until large bubbles form around the handle of a wooden spoon placed in the oil—if the bubbles are small, the oil isn't hot enough.

The method for cooking the jelabi and soaking them in syrup is shown over the page. Repeat the process with the remaining batter and enjoy at room temperature. Jelabi tastes best on the day it's made, but will keep for up to 2 days in an airtight container.

1. Gently but firmly pipe the batter into the oil in a continuous circular motion to form coils.

2. Carefully lift the jelabi out of the oil with a large slotted spoon.

3. Dip the jelabi in the syrup for about 20 seconds, turning so that the syrup is absorbed on both sides.

4. Set aside the syrup-soaked jelabi on a large tray or plate to cool—they can be placed on top of one another while cooling.

Clockwise from top left:
Haft mewa (page 22);
Mahee (page 30);
Kolcheh Nowrozi (page 29);
Challaw (page 111);
Morgh palaw (page 129);
Sabzi (page 25);
Jelabi (page 33);
Maasteh khanagi (page 26)

MANTU

Mantu are small steamed dumplings intricately folded by hand. Because of the labor involved to make them—from rolling out the pastry to filling the dumplings and folding them into flowerbud-like bundles—they are often reserved for special occasions. It is not unusual for family and friends to gather before an event to make mantu together, which is an occasion in itself.

In many ways, mantu captures perfectly the cross-cultural pollination that flourished along the Silk Road. The dish is thought to have originated in Central Asia, in territories belonging to the Mongol Empire, from where it was carried to Turkey. As the recipe's popularity spread, the dish was adapted to create a number of cultural variations, including Turkish manti, Chinese mantou, and Korean mandoo. Each of these iterations follows the same basic formula of hand-rolled dough that's usually filled with ground meat and vegetables, and served topped with a tomato-based sauce and garlic-yogurt dressing.

In this mantu recipe, the dumplings are stuffed with a sautéed onion, cabbage, and carrot filling, then topped with a rich tomato-based lamb kofta sauce or vegetarian sauce, and dotted with chana dal, reflecting the connections between India and Afghanistan. The dish is finished with a generous drizzle of garlic-yogurt dressing, and a sprinkling of dried mint and paprika.

You will need a large steamer pot to steam the mantu. At Parwana, we use a metal steamer—these are available in various sizes from Asian grocery shops. They include a base for the water, several trays with holes that stack on top and a lid. A stacked bamboo steamer could also work.

Lamb kofta sauce (page 46) or vegetarian
   tomato sauce (see page 47)
Dried mint and sweet paprika, to serve
Sunflower oil, for brushing
Salt

FOR THE FILLING
1 carrot, peeled and coarsely chopped
2 yellow onions, coarsely chopped
9 oz (250 g) savoy cabbage,
   coarsely chopped
½ teaspoon coriander seeds, crushed in
   a spice grinder or mortar and pestle
1 teaspoon curry powder
½ teaspoon freshly ground black pepper

FOR THE DOUGH
3½ cups (1 lb/450 g) all-purpose flour
1 tablespoon sunflower oil
1 cup (250 ml) warm water

FOR THE GARLIC-YOGURT DRESSING
½ cup (4½ oz/130 g) plain yogurt
½ teaspoon garlic powder

First make the filling. In a food processor, process the carrot until finely chopped, but not mushy. Place in a medium saucepan and repeat with the onion. Add the onion to the carrot in the saucepan. Process the cabbage to a similar size and add to the pan. Stir in 1 cup (250 ml) water, cover with a lid, and place the saucepan over medium heat.

Cook the vegetables for 15 minutes, or until softened, then drain well in a colander. Transfer to a bowl and add the coriander, curry powder, pepper, and 2 teaspoons salt. Mix thoroughly to combine and set the filling aside to cool completely.

For the dough, combine the flour and 2 teaspoons salt in a large bowl, then add the oil and mix well to combine. Slowly add the water, kneading to incorporate between additions. You may not need it all, but use enough water to form a firm dough. Turn out the dough onto a work surface and knead for 5 minutes, or until it is smooth and elastic. Place in a clean bowl, cover with plastic wrap, and set aside to rest for 15 minutes.

Rolling out the pastry and forming each mantu can be a little tricky and may require some practice to master—but the instructions over the page will take you through the process one step at a time.

Set the finished mantu aside on a tray brushed with oil to prevent sticking and repeat with the remaining filling and wrappers.

To steam the mantu, fill the base of a steamer with water, place the lid on top, and bring to a boil. Brush the steamer trays generously with oil to prevent sticking, then space out the mantu on the trays, without overcrowding them. Stack the trays on top of the base and cover with the lid.

Steam the mantu over medium heat for 35–40 minutes, or until the dough is translucent and completely cooked through.

While the mantu are steaming, prepare the lamb kofta sauce or vegetarian tomato sauce.

To make the yogurt dressing, whisk the yogurt, garlic powder, and ½ teaspoon salt in a small bowl until smooth. Spread half the garlic-yogurt dressing over a large platter and arrange the mantu over the top. Pour over the lamb kofta sauce or vegetarian tomato sauce, then drizzle the remaining garlic-yogurt dressing on top. Sprinkle the mantu with dried mint and paprika, and serve immediately.

1. Roll out the dough to a paper-thin rectangle about 24 in (60 cm) long and 16 in (40 cm) wide.

2. Using a sharp knife, cut vertically into 4 in (10 cm) wide strips.

3. Stack the strips on top of each other.

4. Cut horizontally at 4 in (10 cm) intervals—you should end up with about twenty-four 4 in (10 cm) square mantu wrappers.

5

6

7

8

5. Put a teaspoon of the cooled filling in the center. Dampen the edges, then pick up two diagonally opposite corners.

6. Bring together over the filling and pinch to seal.

7. Repeat with the other two corners so you have a small, sealed square-ish parcel.

8. Place both your middle fingers and thumbs at each end, with your index finger positioned in between. Bring the ends together around your index fingers and pinch to seal. You should end up with an almost-oval parcel with two ends pinched together and two circular openings (where your index fingers were positioned).

Ashak (page 44); opposite: Mantu (page 38)

ASHAK

Ashak, another well-loved dumpling dish of Afghan cuisine, is made using the same dough as mantu (see page 38), but these are less intricate to fold. Typically, they are filled with gandana, a traditional Afghan leek that can be substituted with garlic chives or leeks. Ashak are boiled, then served with lamb kofta sauce or vegetarian tomato sauce and a garlic-yogurt dressing. It's a good idea to have these ready before making ashak, so that when the dumplings are ready, there will be no delay in serving.

Like mantu, ashak is considered a special-occasion dish. Because the dumplings are somewhat time-consuming to make, family and friends often gather together to make them.

2 tablespoons sunflower oil
Lamb kofta sauce (see page 46) or
  vegetarian tomato sauce (see page 47)
1 teaspoon ground turmeric
1 teaspoon dried mint
Salt

FOR THE FILLING
4 cups (1 lb 2 oz/500 g) finely chopped
  garlic chives or leeks
Small handful finely chopped fresh
  cilantro leaves and stalks

FOR THE DOUGH
3½ cups (1 lb/450 g) all-purpose flour
1 tablespoon sunflower oil
1 cup (250 ml) warm water

FOR THE GARLIC-YOGURT DRESSING
½ cup (4½ oz/130 g) plain yogurt
½ teaspoon garlic powder

First make the filling. In a colander, wash the chopped garlic chives thoroughly and allow the excess water to drain. Add 1 tablespoon salt to the chives and mix well with your hands. Take handfuls of the salted chives and squeeze to remove as much liquid as possible, then place in a bowl. Add the cilantro and 1 teaspoon freshly ground black pepper, mix well, and set aside.

For the dough, combine the flour and 2 teaspoons salt in a large bowl, then add the oil and mix well. Slowly add the water, kneading to incorporate between additions. You may not need it all, but use enough water to form a firm dough. Turn out the dough onto a work surface and knead for 5 minutes, or until it is smooth and elastic. Place in a clean bowl, cover with plastic wrap, and set aside to rest for 15 minutes.

When the dough is rested, turn out onto a surface lightly dusted with flour and roll into a paper-thin rectangle about 24 in (60 cm) long and 40 cm (16 in) wide. Using a 2¾ in (7 cm) cookie cutter, or as close to this size as possible, cut as many circles as you can. Leave them flat on the work surface, ready to be filled with the chive filling.

Line a tray or large plate with paper towels and have a small bowl of water on hand. Working with one wrapper at a time, wet the circumference with your finger, being careful not to make the dough soggy, then place a teaspoon of the chive filling in the center. Fold the wrapper in half over the filling to create a semicircle, then pick it up and press the edges firmly together to seal, so it won't open while boiling. Place on the lined tray and repeat with the remaining wrappers and filling. You can place ashak in layers on the same tray, but make sure you place a sheet of paper towel between each layer to prevent sticking.

Three-quarters fill a medium pot with water and bring to a boil. Add 2 teaspoons oil and 1 teaspoon salt. Carefully add the ashak to the boiling water and stir occasionally for 6–7 minutes, or until the dough is translucent. Using a slotted spoon, gently remove the ashak, allowing the water to drain well, and place on a plate.

To make the garlic-yogurt dressing, whisk the yogurt, garlic powder, and ½ teaspoon salt in a small bowl until smooth. Spread half the dressing over a large platter and arrange the ashak on top. Pour over the lamb kofta sauce or vegetarian tomato sauce, then drizzle with the remaining garlic-yogurt dressing.

Place a small frying pan over high heat. Add the remaining 1 tablespoon oil, along with the turmeric and dried mint. Heat for 1–2 minutes, or until the oil is hot and infused with the turmeric and mint. Carefully pour the hot infused oil over the ashak and serve immediately.

LAMB KOFTA SAUCE

کوفته پاکستان

2 large, ripe tomatoes, quartered
2½ tablespoons sunflower oil
1 large yellow onion, finely chopped
1 garlic clove, crushed
1 lb 2 oz (500 g) ground lamb
1 teaspoon ground turmeric
1 teaspoon curry powder
1 teaspoon coriander seeds, crushed in
  a spice grinder or mortar and pestle
2½ tablespoons tomato paste
1 teaspoon white vinegar
¼ cup (2 oz/60 g) chana dal
  (split chickpeas)
Salt

Many dishes in Afghan cooking require the layering of sauces and dairy-based dressings. This kofta sauce, typically made using lamb, is a flavor-rich topping for dumplings such as mantu (see page 38) and ashak (see page 44), or it can be stirred through aush soup (see page 224). Onion and garlic are browned for the base, to which the ground meat is added and fried. Plenty of tomato creates a rich sauce flavored with fragrant spices.

In a blender or food processor, process the tomatoes until puréed and set aside.

Add the oil to a medium saucepan over medium heat. Fry the onion and garlic for 3–4 minutes, or until golden brown, then add the meat and fry for 10 minutes or so, stirring frequently with a wooden spoon and breaking it up so there are no large clumps, until the meat is browned.

Stir in the turmeric, curry powder, coriander, and 1 teaspoon salt and fry for another 5 minutes, or until the meat starts to release water. Boil the mixture for a further 5 minutes, so that some of the water reduces and the oil rises to the top.

Stir in the tomatoes, tomato paste, vinegar, and 1 cup (250 ml) water. Continue to break down any remaining large clumps of meat with a wooden spoon, so it's relatively evenly ground, and bring to a boil.

Cover the saucepan with a lid and simmer gently over low heat for 10 minutes, or until the sauce has reduced and thickened.

Meanwhile, put the chana dal into a small saucepan with enough water to cover. Bring to a boil and cook for 10 minutes, or until the dal is soft, but not mushy. Drain, then add to the sauce and stir through to combine.

VEGETARIAN TOMATO SAUCE

رُب بادنجان روی

This sauce is a vegetarian substitute for lamb kofta sauce (see opposite) and is served over dumplings such as mantu (see page 38) and ashak (see page 44), or on top of aush soup (see page 224). It is suitable for both vegetarian and vegan diets, adding layers of flavor and richness to the dumpling dishes.

½ cup (125 ml) sunflower oil
1 large yellow onion, finely chopped
1 moderately hot fresh red chili, finely chopped
4 garlic cloves, crushed
1 teaspoon curry powder
1 teaspoon ground red pepper
2 large tomatoes, finely diced
1 tablespoon white vinegar
1 teaspoon white sugar
¼ cup (2 oz/60 g) chana dal (split chickpeas)
Salt

Add the oil to a medium saucepan over medium heat. Fry the onion, chopped chili, and garlic for 2–3 minutes, or until golden brown. Next, add the curry powder, ground red pepper, and 1 teaspoon salt, and fry for a further 2 minutes, or until fragrant. Stir in the tomatoes and cook for 10 minutes, or until the tomatoes soften. Add 1½ cups (375 ml) water and bring to a boil over high heat, then add the vinegar and sugar. Reduce the heat to medium and simmer for another 15 minutes, or until the sauce has reduced and thickened, and is bright red in color.

Meanwhile, add the chana dal to a small saucepan with enough water to cover. Bring to a boil and cook for about 10 minutes, or until the dal is soft, but not mushy. Drain, then add to the sauce and stir through to combine.

BOLANI

بولانی

3¾ cups (1 lb 1 oz/485 g) all-purpose
 flour
1½ teaspoons instant yeast
1½ cups (375 ml) lukewarm water
1 tablespoon sunflower oil, plus extra
 for frying
Fillings of choice (see pages 52-53)
Salt

Bolani are delicious hand-rolled flatbreads, stuffed with various fillings, then pan-fried golden brown and crisp.

Like the hand-formed dumpling dishes of mantu (see page 38) and ashak (see page 44), bolani are typically made with family and friends, and eaten straight off the tawah (a traditional flat iron frying pan) as they cook, while more are made hot and fresh, until everyone has had their fill. Bolani are eaten by tearing off strips and dipping them into a relish, such as chutney morcheh sorkh (see page 87), plain thick yogurt, or jaan-e-ama yogurt dip (see page 191). Afghans also like to eat this savory treat with a cup of sweet tea.

For the various fillings, see pages 52–53. It's important to have your chosen fillings prepared before rolling out the dough and a good time to do this is while the dough is resting.

In a medium bowl, stir the flour, yeast, and 2 teaspoons salt to combine. Create a well in the center and slowly add only enough warm water to just wet the ingredients, mixing with your hands in a circular motion to distribute evenly, then add the oil. While continuously mixing, slowly add the remaining water (you might not need it all, only enough to form a firm dough) and knead until the dough is firm. You may need to slightly adjust the amount of water or flour to achieve the right consistency.

Shape the dough into a ball, place in an oiled bowl, cover with a tea towel, and set aside to rest for about 30 minutes, or until doubled in size.

Divide the dough into 6 equal-sized portions and shape each into a small ball with your hands. Place them on a tray lined with parchment paper with 2 in (5 cm) between them, cover with a tea towel, and set aside to rest for another 10 minutes, or until doubled in size.

On a lightly floured surface, roll out one ball of dough into a circle 4–4½ in (10–12 cm) in diameter. It might take a bit of practice to roll it evenly into a perfect circle, but working from the center outwards is generally a good technique to achieve the right shape. Once rolled, place 4 tablespoons of filling on one half of the circle and spread it evenly to cover half, leaving a ½ in (1 cm) border. Fold the other half over the filling to form a semicircle and press the edges together to seal. Repeat with the remaining dough and filling.

Add enough oil to cover the base of a tawah, griddle, or heavy-based frying pan, and heat over high heat. In batches, lift the bolani carefully into the pan and fry, turning once, for 4 minutes each side, or until golden brown and crisp.

Transfer to a board lined with paper towels to soak up any extra oil, then serve immediately with chutney and/or yogurt for dipping.

GANDANA BOLANI FILLING

2 cups (9 oz/250 g) finely chopped
   garlic chives
Large handful fresh cilantro, leaves and
   stalks finely chopped
½ cup (1¾ oz/50 g) scallions, thinly
   sliced
1 small yellow onion, finely chopped
1 teaspoon coriander seeds, crushed in
   a spice grinder or mortar and pestle
1 teaspoon ground red pepper
1 tablespoon sunflower oil
Salt and freshly ground black pepper

This filling traditionally uses gandana, a type of leek found throughout Afghanistan, which is a popular filling for bolani. My grandfather, who was an avid lover of gardening and homegrown produce, grew his own gandana. The vegetable isn't easily found outside the region, however, so Afghans living around the world often substitute garlic chives, which have a similar texture and taste.

In a bowl, mix the garlic chives, cilantro, scallions, and onion to combine. Add the spices with 2 teaspoons salt and 1 teaspoon freshly ground black pepper, and mix well. Stir in the oil and set aside until you are ready to fill the bolani.

FILLS 6 BOLANI   *POTATO FLATBREAD STUFFING*

KACHALOO BOLANI FILLING

1 lb 12 oz (800 g) all-purpose potatoes
1 large yellow onion, finely chopped
2 teaspoons coriander seeds, crushed in
   a spice grinder or mortar and pestle
2 teaspoons garlic powder
1 teaspoon ground red pepper
Salt and freshly ground black pepper

Boil the potatoes in a medium saucepan of water for 15 minutes, or until soft when pierced. Set aside to cool, then peel the potatoes and mash in a large bowl. Add the onion, spices, 2 teaspoons salt, 1 teaspoon freshly ground black pepper, and 2½ tablespoons water, and mix to combine well. Set aside until you are ready to fill the bolani.

CHICKEN FLATBREAD STUFFING

MORGH KOFTA BOLANI FILLING

کوفته مرغ

2½ tablespoons sunflower oil
1 large yellow onion, finely chopped
14 oz (400 g) ground chicken, preferably
  leg and thigh meat
1 teaspoon garlic powder
1 teaspoon ground red pepper
1 teaspoon coriander seeds, crushed in
  a spice grinder or mortar and pestle
Salt and freshly ground black pepper

Add the oil to a medium saucepan over high heat and fry the onion until golden. Add the ground chicken, spices, 2 teaspoons salt, and 1 teaspoon black pepper, and stir to combine well. Fry for 10 minutes, or until the chicken is cooked through, but not overly browned. Drain any excess oil from the mixture in a colander and set aside until you are ready to fill the bolani.

PUMPKIN FLATBREAD STUFFING

KADOO BOLANI FILLING

کدو

14 oz (400 g) winter squash, such as
  kabocha or acorn, seeded, peeled
  and cut into ½ in (1 cm) cubes
½ cup (125 ml) warm water
1 garlic clove, crushed
1 teaspoon coriander seeds, crushed in
  a spice grinder or mortar and pestle
Salt and freshly ground black pepper

Place the squash and water in a small saucepan and cook over low heat for 15 minutes, or until the squash is soft and the water has been completely absorbed. Mash the squash in a bowl with the garlic, coriander, 1 teaspoon freshly ground black pepper, and 1½ teaspoons salt, and mix the ingredients together well. Set aside until you are ready to fill the bolani.

Making Bolani (page 48), with Gandana, Kachaloo, and Kadoo fillings (pages 52–53)

Chapter 2

Roots & Belonging

فصل دوم

AFGHANISTAN EMERGES
FROM THE MISTS OF HISTORY

فضل رحیم

Love of a Nation

"By blood, we are immersed in love of you.
The youth lose their heads for your sake.
I come to you and my heart finds rest.
Away from you, grief clings to my heart like a snake.
I forget the throne of Delhi
when I remember the mountain tops of my beautiful Pakhtunkhwa.
If I must choose between the world and you,
I shall not hesitate to claim your barren deserts as my own."

Ahmad Shah Durrani, "the father of Afghanistan"

The story of Afghanistan in the nineteenth century is influenced by the convergence of two disparate, and often conflicting, plot lines—the attempt by Britain to retain and strengthen its empire, and the rise of Russia. For the lands sandwiched ominously between these northern empires and their jealously pursued southern prizes of Persia and India, this often meant trouble. Forebodingly, in the 1800s Afghanistan shared borders with both India and Persia, while a newly confident Russia loomed above it like a storm cloud. Afghanistan was, unsurprisingly, to become embroiled in a competitive jostle between Britain and Russia, referred to by the British as the "Great Game." In Afghanistan this played out at first as a gentlemanly and somewhat restrained attempt by both powers to win over the Emir, Dost Mohammad Khan, but eventually descended into conflict.

At the same time that the Great Game was forcibly played out as foreign policy across the lands of Afghanistan, a localized sense of identity and power was also brewing. In the years preceding this foreign struggle, the eighteenth century had brought forth a galvanized sense of "Afghan-ness" that was slowly emerging from the cocoon of history in which it had crystallized. This unique cauldron of cultures and disparate genetics had finally bubbled into something more consolidated when viewed through the long focusing lens of the past. From the eighteenth to the twentieth century, as the concept of the "modern nation" evolved globally, Afghanistan's own sense of existence would further

develop—and food, culture, and kinship all played a part in catalyzing and defining this evolution. Despite, or perhaps because of, the foreign occupation of Afghanistan during the nineteenth century, independence, culture, and tradition took on a sense of preciousness. There were glimmers of hope that the image of Afghanistan, untouched by the ambitions of others, could emerge in accordance with its own traditions and potential. In this era the food of Afghanistan became further embedded in, and expressed through, a sense of national identity. Perhaps—before the mass exodus of its population and culture that was to take place in the late twentieth century—this moment marks the high point in the story of Afghan food and its cultivation, at least on its traditional lands. It was during this period too that the less fleeting memories of figures and events that would shape the course of my mother's life, and nurture her passion for cooking, begin to emerge from my family narrative.

My grandparents were born during an era of relatively stable monarchy, progress, and reform. My mother was born and spent her adolescence during the 40-year reign of King Zahir Shah, who would prove to be the last monarch of Afghanistan. Unfolding within the grand and larger-than-life history and landscape of Afghanistan, her childhood was memorable. Everything new in the Afghan world took on its own form, as it was forged through the pressure of the ancient and significant history that preceded it and the geography that surrounded it—both of which would perpetually shape the character and faces of its people. Old tribal affiliations—although ever present and influential—were being managed into a new world by some of Afghanistan's most progressive and enlightened leaders. Islam was being reconciled with modernity at a constitutional level; there were family picnics at the foot of the Hindu Kush and in ancient gardens with crystal-clear brooks, and investment in education—in my mother's family, particularly in literature and philosophy.

Durr-i-Durran: the "pearl of pearls"

One of the first steps towards a more distinctly Afghan identity had taken place in 1709, when native Pashtun tribesmen, led by Mirwais Hotak, overthrew Persian Safavid and Indian Mughal rule from their base in Qandahar in Afghanistan. The Hotak Empire then spread across parts of Afghanistan, and through modern-day Iran, Tajikistan, and Turkmenistan. By 1738, however, Afghanistan was wrestled back under Persian control by Nader Shah Afshar, the Shah of Persia. Nader Shah, who with his easy conquest of Mughal India had become one of the most powerful

Persian Shahs, but was becoming increasingly cruel and despotic as he rose, was assassinated in 1747, most likely by his own men.

There were those loyal to Nader Shah who lamented his death. This included Ahmad Shah Durrani, a tribal Pashtun of Afghan origin, who had risen from political prisoner to one of Nader Shah's most trusted generals, leading a cavalry of thousands of men. Upon Nader Shah's murder, the tribal chieftains of Afghanistan decided that the time had come to choose a new ruler from among their own. With Persia riddled with internal strife and the power of the once mighty Mughals in India waning, the moment had arrived for Afghanistan to develop its own identity. Durrani, reserved and unassuming, had not put his name forward as a claimant to the throne and was perhaps not the most obvious choice of leader from among the chieftains. Yet he was named the worthiest candidate by a mystic seer, who saw something unique in his character. The chieftains accepted without opposition and in 1747 the 25-year-old Durrani was crowned Emir of Afghanistan. As King of the Afghans, he became

known as the durr-i-durran, or the "pearl of pearls." This was, in hindsight, a historic moment in the trajectory of Afghanistan. Durrani's greatest gift was his ability to unite the region's various tribes, including numerous Pashtuns, Tajiks, and other Persians who remained in Afghanistan, as Qandahar, Ghazni, Herat, Kabul and Persian territory, including Nishapur and Mughal territory west of the Indus River, ceded to his control. Never intending to seize the entirety of India, he refused to penetrate further into its lands, thus avoiding confrontation with the British East India Company and allowing its full acquisition of Bengal by the late eighteenth century.

When Durrani died in 1772, the last empire of Afghanistan quickly splintered again into a number of smaller states in the jostle for power. His son and heir, Timur Shah, transferred the capital to Kabul from Qandahar in a bid to thwart conspirators for the throne. It was not enough, and what followed was a fast-moving political struggle, ending with the ascension of Dost Mohammad Khan of the Barakzai clan in 1823, which coincided with British and Russian intervention. However, during his reign as Emir, Durrani had managed to cultivate and then kindle a sense of national consciousness unlike any previous leader. He was the predecessor of the contemporary concept of Afghanistan—its father.

The demise of the Silk Road and the clash of rising empires

Afghanistan's sense of nationhood was emerging against the backdrop of three major global changes that were unfolding. The center of gravity had shifted from the East to the West during the fifteenth and sixteenth centuries, when Spain and Portugal's maritime expeditions opened up much of the world to Europe. Then, within Europe, during the seventeenth and eighteenth centuries the British and Dutch transformed themselves into the new world powers as the Iberian influence faded. Thirdly, during the nineteenth century, Russia emerged as a rising empire.

For the Silk Road, and the many towns and cities on its routes that had glimmered as jewels of the ancient world, it was not only the advent of maritime trading that spelled the end of prosperity. On the contrary, the beginning of oceanic trade gave some of the cities across Central Asia and India a new burst of life as the influx of currency into Europe was transferred to the East to purchase the many goods the West was increasingly hungry for. As late as the eighteenth century, huge volumes of textiles and other precious goods made their way over the land routes of antiquity from India to Persia. Kabul was also still an important trading center, where large numbers of caravans met to buy and sell thoroughbred horses, textiles, spices, and other luxury items. The pattern of prosperity changed most with the passing of much of India into British hands, making many of the overland trading routes redundant. European evolutions in military warfare reduced the importance of cavalry—something the empires and trading posts along the Silk Road had long thrived on—and shifted power squarely westwards. Central Asia was fading as a center of cultural splendor.

Compounding this decline, during the nineteenth century, Russia was on the rise in the north of the Eurasian steppes, subsuming the grassy plains that had once been the territories of the Mongol Empire. Its rise was made possible by the military revolution— the diminished importance of cavalry starved the nomadic tribes of their source of power. Many tribes were also unable to keep apace with the technological advances in heavy artillery and the new machines of warfare in the way that settled societies could. For the first time in history the balance of power shifted from the nomadic people of the steppes—who, through their fierce swordsmanship and expert horse-wielding, had for centuries contained the empires they surrounded—to settled, agrarian societies.

Both China and Russia acquired lands until their borders almost touched, but Russia benefitted the most. The vast swathes of mineral-rich loess-soiled plains were transformed from pastoral land into fertile and high-yielding farmland—endless fields of golden wheat. This agricultural boom, alongside the reduced cost of protection needed against nomadic warriors, enabled Russia's transformation into a superpower.

For Britain, the rise of Russia was not good news. With important and long-cultivated interests in the East—notably India and Persia—to protect, the encroaching territorial expansion of another power was met with alarm. Over the following century, the future of the entire region was crystallized in the reality of a looming superpower to the north, and a powerful British India, guarding and growing its commercial and political interests to the south.

The Great Game unfolded in Afghanistan predominantly as a series of Anglo-Afghan wars. The first, fought from 1839 to 1842, was triggered by Russia's encouragement of Persia in its attempt to take Herat. The British intervened, deposed the Afghan Emir, Dost Mohammad Khan, and installed a puppet ruler, Shah Shujah of the Durrani clan. This was never fully accepted as legitimate by the Afghan people and what ensued was a disastrous military campaign for the British, who retreated with heavy losses, paving the way for Russia to become even further entrenched in Persia and Afghanistan.

The second war, from 1878 to 1880, was triggered when Emir Sher Ali Khan (Dost Mohammad's son) met with an uninvited Russian delegation, but refused an audience with the British, and then ignored the subsequent British demand for an apology. This led to the British again stationing troops on Afghan soil.

It was during this second war that the Treaty of Gandamak was signed by Sher Ali Khan's son, Yaqub Khan, while his father was away seeking support in Russia. It effectively allowed Britain to control Afghanistan through regulating its political and commercial interests, and it would come to be considered one of the most humiliating agreements for Afghan sovereignty.

The third war, in 1919, was sparked by Emir Amanullah Khan (great grandson of Dost Mohammad Khan) demanding independence for Afghanistan. He was ultimately successful, with the signing of the Treaty of Rawalpindi affording Afghanistan its independence from British foreign policy in 1919.

Foreign power hits home

The way in which the Great Game played out in Afghanistan was, of course, driven and shaped by various other interests and ebbs and flows in global power during the nineteenth and early twentieth centuries. It rose from the ashes of the Napoleonic Wars, was connected to the diminishing rule of the Ottoman Empire and was influenced by rising tensions with an increasingly powerful Germany, all of which contributed to the tense global atmosphere that led to World War One.

The foreign, distant, and self-serving nature of the Great Game perhaps resonated little with ordinary Afghans, but they were, in at least two ways, forced to pay attention. Firstly, their leaders were installed and deposed on the whim of occupying empires; secondly, national boundaries were drawn that were designed to satiate the appetites of Britain and Russia—the two separate "spheres of influence"—but which cut through and tore apart millennia of tribal, linguistic,

and spiritual homelands. To create a buffer zone, intended to protect imperial interests in the south, in 1893 the British drew the Durand Line, cutting through ancient tribal regions and splitting them across countries into what is now Pakistan. The cost was borne by the Pashtun tribes.

In the north, an awkward boundary line was drawn to demarcate British-controlled Afghan territory from Russian Turkestan—now Afghan and Tajik Badakhshan—which literally split families, communities, and trade relationships on two sides of the Panj River. It was this same river, known then as the Oxus, that Alexander the Great had crossed with his men in the fourth century BC, and from this region in the north-east that Genghis Khan's tribes crossed into Afghanistan in the thirteenth century in their consolidation of the largest land empire the world had seen. In accordance with the boundary drawn in 1893, the region was now controlled by Russia and, during the Bolshevik Revolution, which was to take place in 1917 and give rise to the Soviet Union, differences in life across the river, and border, would become ever more stark.

An oasis in time and place

It was during this period of the Great Game that my maternal great-grandfather, Azrat Shah Pachah Sahib Tigiri, was born in the province of Laghman in 1870. He was 23 when the boundaries that exist to this day were drawn around Afghanistan. His life path took a spiritual route, leading him to the role of a Sufi pir, or leader.

Sufism is the same mystical strain of Islam that had been practiced for centuries by the poets and saints, such as Rumi, and which speckles the history of the East. Sufism is not dogmatic but, instead, enshrined in the idea that the greatest struggles are directed inwards in the quest to emancipate oneself from an untamed ego. It is the undertone of the type of Islam that had long prevailed in Afghanistan, which had always tempered overly zealous religious ideologies from spreading too far and helped to retain a sense of balance in the Islam practiced in the region—but which would, by the twentieth century, be eclipsed by the emergence of religion that was far more radicalized.

Pachah Sahib died in 1918, the year before Afghanistan, under the rule of Amanullah Khan, won its independence from a Britain wearied by World War One.

Pachah Sahib was married to my great-grandmother, Bibi Hawa, and together they had five children. The year he died, she was pregnant with their final child—Hamida, my grandmother, who would never meet her father. Bibi Hawa was an enlightened force who shaped the ideologies and norms that would largely influence my mother's life. A widely respected and revered woman, she took control of all affairs on the death of her husband. She ensured that her children were all raised with a keen sense of their identity and organized for a renowned cook, whom they referred to as Aapa, to be the chef in her home, ensuring that all her children were taught to prepare Afghan food from one of the best. There is a story that senior ministers of the Afghan government would call at her house, requesting Aapa prepare his famous palaw rice, the

They grew up during the reign of Amanullah Khan, the great reformer who realized the moment was ripe after 1919 to modernize Afghanistan, newly liberated from foreign influence, on its own terms. Somewhat insidiously, it was this very openness to adopting Western ideals that would later eclipse and undermine Afghanistan's own rich and complex history. But during the early 1900s, reform was being enshrined in a way that recognized the interconnected nature of culture and was pursued in the spirit of adapting to the times, while still being guided by the norms indigenous to the region. Importantly, the process was still being steered by Afghanistan's own, whose views had been incubated during a time when a mix of history, progressive ideals, and enlightenment was steering the country forward.

Bibi Hamida Ghafour
(نجف، حمیده)

Abdul Ghafour Khan and children (including Farida, first from left)
(عبدالغفور خان)

taste of which they insisted they could not forget. She also organized for her children to be tutored by the finest scholarly minds to open up their worlds.

Hamida was closest to and shared a special bond with her oldest brother, Shamsuddin Majrooh, who would go on to become the Chair of the Council and one of the five people who drafted the nation's 1964 constitution. This was a constitution that sought to reconcile Islamic principles and Western democratic ideals, which the drafters considered need not be mutually exclusive.

Cast in the image of their mother's bright aura, the children were products of a nation given the chance to flourish. They were progressive and enlightened minds, forged during an oasis in time in Afghanistan.

A life of love
In her late twenties, Hamida married my grandfather, Abdul Ghafour Khan, who was also from a notable family of the Laghman province. They were deeply in love, and my mother recalls her parents' open affection for one another. When my grandfather, a dashing and rising military star, left on assignment, my grandmother would write love poetry to him. Bibi Hamida Ghafour had a flair for language and poetry; her poetry, written in her native Pashto, and her writing would be recognized in publications across the nation. After her early death in 1960, at the age of 42, she would continue to be honored in literary circles. In one article, Benawah, the minister for media and himself a renowned writer, wrote: "Lady Hamida is the intelligent daughter of Pachah Sahib Tigiri …

In writing poetry, she was fluent and wrote with ease … Her poetry is dedicated to the love of her nation and reflects a profound love for her people … Her poetry speaks about her own destiny, and much of it is also directed at alleviating the subjugated position of Afghan women … Her poetry is sweet and smooth, and reveals her desire for the independence, progress, and freedom of her country. The combination of her profound views and her talent makes her a highly ranked writer of the nation."

Foreseeing the harm that the unrelenting tribal factionalism slowly spreading through the country would create for her beloved nation, a few lines of one of my grandmother's poems read:

The eyes of the spring cloud
Became wet
Weeping for the state of nature it finds you in

It was indeed this tribalism that jarred the progress of the nation. Amanullah Khan's reforms were largely accepted in the cities, but too much for some others to handle—he introduced a new Afghan currency and built hospitals, orphanages, communications networks, and schools, but also included the removal of the need for women to cover in public, a reform intended to allow women more autonomy over their lives. In the countryside, where tribal customs ran deeper, the changes presented to the mullahs and chieftains were too much too soon; Amanullah had not carried out the necessary political overtures required to get them on his side. Following an uprising led by the countryside, Amanullah fled the country in 1929 and died in exile in 1960—a tragic loss of potential for the nation.

It was that same year my grandmother died, leaving five children under the age of nine; my mother was just four. She recalls being too young to understand that her mother had passed, only crying softly at night from missing her deeply and wondering where she had gone. My mother's childhood unfolded during the reign of Zahir Shah, another descendant of Dost Mohammad Khan. Zahir Shah's rule started suddenly: his father, Nadir Shah, king after the ousting of Amanullah Khan, was assassinated four short years into his reign, and the young prince, aged nineteen, assumed the throne. He would prove to be a just and relatively moderate ruler, who persisted with modernization and reform, but in a way—for better or worse—that was less antagonistic to tribal chieftains of the provinces. In this era, which would turn out to be that of the final monarch, my mother and her siblings

were lovingly and dotingly raised by their father, who remained deeply affected by the loss of the love of his life until his own death. He treasured the joy of cooking he had been given by his wife, taught to her through the determination of her own mother. He was an accomplished and natural cook, making his own fig jam, preserves, and flatbreads. A lover of gardens, like the great Emperor Babur in Kabul centuries earlier, he cultivated beautiful lawns and fruit orchards and grew his own produce. He planted apricot, apple, and pear trees, mostly for the beauty of their blossoms. He cultivated roses, lilacs, and the famous magenta-leaved arghawan, which also stud the gardens of Babur. He grew tomatoes, mint, cilantro, gandana, chives, cucumbers, and other vegetables—native ingredients which would be used when preparing feasts. My mother recalls the merging of these two great loves—her father preparing food, such as kebabs over hot coals during the celebration of Eid, outdoors in the gardens he cared for so deeply.

This love for the culinary, and for the beauty and cohesion that came with food, spread like a fever into the emerging character of my mother. From a young age she loved to cook and learned hungrily from the accomplished chefs who were brought in to prepare the best of Afghan food for hundreds of guests at grand parties and festivities. Valuing food—and the culture and tradition that came with it—was an art and pursuit passed down the generations from the time of Bibi Hawa to my mother.

It wouldn't be long before the years of cultural flourishing were compromised, in some ways by the necessity of a small landlocked country trying to keep up with the spinning wheel of modernity, and in others by the more self-serving reasons of its own leaders. The end of this era of Afghan independence would also coincide with the end of the period of belonging and connection to land that fluttered through my mother's adolescence like an ephemeral dream.

This chapter includes recipes relating to two significant themes of this time in my mother's life: food made during the day trips and picnics that stud her early memories and which reflect a time in Afghanistan's history when it was trying to develop a sense of culture on its own terms; and food made for commemoration, as would have been made at the time of my foremothers' and forefathers' passing.

TOKHME BANJANROMI

تخم بادنجان رومی دار

1 cup (250 ml) sunflower oil
1 large yellow onion, halved and
  thinly sliced
2 garlic cloves, thinly sliced
3 ripe tomatoes, halved and thinly sliced
1 moderately hot fresh red chili,
  thinly sliced
4 large eggs
1 teaspoon ground red pepper
Coarsely chopped fresh cilantro leaves,
  to serve
Salt

This recipe is for traditional Afghan-style breakfast eggs, which are cooked in a sauce of onion, tomatoes, and chili, absorbing the complementary flavors. As with most Afghan meals, particularly breakfast, fresh naan breads (see pages 82 and 83) served on the side are essential. Afghan breakfast spreads also typically include shir chai (see page 218), a traditional milk tea that, with its dairy base, provides a calorie- and protein-rich start to the day.

My mother recalls having this dish for breakfast during family day trips, such as to Mazar-i-Sharif for the red tulip festival during the spring equinox. It would be made in a beautiful copper karayee, a shallow, heavy-based pan used in Afghan cooking. The karayee would be placed directly over a portable kerosene burner, where the eggs, vegetables, and spices would bubble away. The large karayee was then placed in the middle of the breakfast spread, surrounded by naans and various chais, for everyone to help themselves.

This is an easy dish to scale up, to feed as many guests as you need.

Heat the oil in a medium saucepan over high heat and fry the onion and garlic for 5 minutes, or until softened and browned. Add the tomatoes and fresh chili, and cook, stirring occasionally, until the tomatoes have softened, but are still intact, then mix in 2 teaspoons salt, or to taste.

Break the eggs into a bowl then pour evenly over the tomato and onion mixture in the saucepan. Break up the yolks gently, if that's how you prefer them, then cover the pan with a lid. Reduce the heat to low and cook the eggs slowly, shaking the pan occasionally to avoid sticking, for 5–10 minutes for soft, 10–15 minutes for medium-soft, or until the eggs are cooked to your liking. Sprinkle with 1 teaspoon freshly ground black pepper, the ground red pepper, and cilantro, and serve hot—straight from the pan.

KEBABEH SIKHI

کباب سیخی

While the type of kebab many people associate with Afghan cuisine is lamb or chicken threaded onto skewers and cooked over coals, there are in fact a number of different ways to prepare kebabs, as you will see throughout this chapter.

Some kebabs, such as kebabeh sikhi, are cooked over hot coals, some are cooked along with a selection of vegetables and spices, while others are shaped into round or oblong patties and fried. That said, all kebabs are commonly enjoyed with an array of chutneys, relishes, vegetables, and fresh, hot naans.

This recipe is for skewered lamb kebabs cooked over charcoal, the type my grandfather would make with meat from the qurbani, the animal sacrifice made for Eid al-Fitr. My mother recalls that during Eid, the celebration that follows Ramadan, the month of fasting observed by Muslims, her father would, after distributing meat to the needy, relatives, and friends, set some aside to make these kebabs for his family.

She remembers her father preparing the meat outdoors, skewering pieces to cook over hot coals in the garden. She remembers the sharp but warm aroma of the spices and meat crackling together and fusing with the scent of the coals, luring all the children out to take part. The joy of food for her father, she says, stemmed not only from melding ingredients and flavors, but also from his belief in the nurturing power of food, and how it became amplified when people came together to eat among the rows of lilacs, roses, and poplars so lovingly cultivated in his garden.

Begin preparing this dish the day before you would like to serve it, to marinate the meat and soak wooden skewers, if you're using them, in water. Soaking the skewers prevents them from burning.

2 large onions, coarsely chopped
2 moderately hot fresh red chilies, coarsely chopped
2 garlic cloves, coarsely chopped
4½ lb (2 kg) diced lamb leg
Heaped 1 tablespoon coriander seeds, crushed
4 tablespoons sunflower oil
Naan flatbread (page 82), lime wedges, thinly sliced red onion, and fresh herbs, to serve
Salt and freshly ground black pepper

Blend the onion, chili, garlic, and ½ cup (125 ml) water to a fine pulp in a food processor. Lay a piece of cheesecloth over the top of a large bowl and strain the mixture through it, pressing to extract as much liquid as possible, and discarding the solids. Add the lamb to the strained marinade in the bowl, then add the coriander, 2 tablespoons salt, 2 teaspoons freshly ground black pepper, and the oil. Mix well to combine and coat the meat, cover, and marinate in the fridge overnight.

This type of kebab is best grilled on a charcoal barbecue. When you are ready to cook the kebabeh sikhi, start by preheating the coals; the coals should be evenly glowing orange before you begin cooking.

Thread the marinated lamb pieces closely onto metal or pre-soaked wooden skewers, leaving little space between each piece. Place them on the grill over the coals and turn occasionally for 7 minutes, or until both sides are evenly cooked. Be careful not to let the meat dry out or become too crisp on the outside through overcooking. Test a piece of lamb to ensure it's cooked through but tender.

Serve with naan flatbread, lime wedges, thinly sliced red onion, and fresh herbs for brightness and crunch. Add some chutney (see pages 86 and 87) on the side for a burst of acidity and heat.

DU PYAZA

دوپیازه

1 small red onion, sliced into rings
½ cup (125 ml) white vinegar
1 lb 2 oz (500 g) lamb shanks, bone in,
   cut into 4 pieces
1 large yellow onion, coarsely chopped
1 teaspoon ground turmeric
½ cup (4 oz/113 g) yellow split peas,
   soaked in warm water for 4 hours
1 naan flatbread (see page 82)
1 small handful fresh mint leaves
Salt and freshly ground black pepper

This is a lamb kebab dish that my mother remembers preparing for family picnics in such places as the valleys beneath the Hindu Kush mountains for the Meleh Golghondi—a festival that honors the fleeting, but striking, week-long bloom of the fuchsia-leaved arghawan trees.

Like the scenery, this dish, with its contrasting colors and textures, is a favorite in Afghan cuisine for its striking presentation, and forms a beautiful centerpiece on any Afghan table.

As is common in Afghan cooking, a pressure cooker is used here to cut down the time it takes to tenderize the meat, and also to evenly cook the ingredients. If you don't have one, use a large saucepan, but allow an hour or so to cook the meat. You'll also need to soak the split peas for a few hours before you start.

Combine the red onion and vinegar in a small bowl and set aside for 1 hour or so to lightly pickle. This will be used as a garnish later.

Place the lamb shanks in a pressure cooker with the yellow onion, turmeric, a heaped 1 tablespoon salt, and 3½ cups (875ml) water, secure the lid, and place over high heat. Once it reaches high pressure, reduce the heat to medium to stabilize the pressure and cook for 25 minutes.

Remove the meat and add the yellow split peas to the pressure cooker. Bring to a boil, uncovered, over high heat, then reduce the heat to low and simmer for 10 minutes, or until the split peas are soft and completely cooked.

To serve, lay the flatbread on a platter. Arrange the lamb pieces on top, spoon over the split peas, and garnish generously with pickled red onion, mint, and freshly ground black pepper. Tear off bite-sized pieces of naan with lamb and split peas and enjoy.

Naan-e roghani (page 83)

KEBABEH DEGEE MORGH

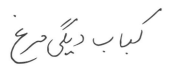

1 cup (250 ml) sunflower oil
2¼ lb (1 kg) chicken thighs and
  drumsticks, bones in, skin removed
2 ripe tomatoes, puréed in a blender
1 teaspoon coriander seeds, crushed in
  a spice grinder or mortar and pestle
1 teaspoon cumin seeds, crushed in a
  spice grinder or mortar and pestle
1 teaspoon fenugreek seeds, crushed in
  a spice grinder or mortar and pestle
1 teaspoon nigella seeds
2 teaspoons grated fresh ginger
2 teaspoons grated garlic
2 moderately hot fresh red chilies,
  thinly sliced
½ cup (4½ oz/130 g) plain yogurt
1 naan flatbread (see page 82)
Fresh long green chili, halved
  lengthways, and lime wedges, to serve
Salt

My mother learned to make this kebab dish as a teenager, from a chef who was invited to her family home to cook for a special occasion, to which many guests had been invited. He wouldn't allow anyone into the kitchen while he prepared the food with some of his juniors alongside, but sensed that my mother was keen to watch and eager to learn. He taught her the importance of choosing the right blend of spices to create balanced and aromatic, but not overpowering, flavors.

Heat the oil in a large wok over high heat. When the oil is hot, carefully place the chicken in the pan and cook, turning occasionally for 10 minutes, or until golden brown. Add the tomatoes, along with 1 tablespoon salt, the crushed spices, nigella seeds, ginger, garlic, sliced chilies, and yogurt. Mix to coat the chicken and combine, then reduce the heat to medium. Cook for 15 minutes, or until the chicken is cooked through and no longer pink inside when cut, and a thickened sauce has formed.

Serve the chicken and sauce over naan flatbread with green chili and lime wedges.

MORGH LAWANG

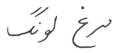

½ cup (4 oz/113 g) yellow split peas
1 cup (250 ml) sunflower oil
3 lb 5 oz (1.5 kg) whole chicken,
  skin removed, cut into 8 pieces
1 large yellow onion, finely diced
3 garlic cloves, finely chopped
Heaped 1 tablespoon grated fresh ginger
3 moderately hot fresh red chilies,
  thinly sliced
½ cup (4½ oz/130 g) plain yogurt
2 teaspoons ground turmeric
2 large ripe tomatoes, finely diced
1 lime or lemon, thinly sliced
½ red onion, thinly sliced
2½ tablespoons fresh cilantro leaves
Salt and freshly ground black pepper

This is a chicken kebab dish called a lawang because of the richly flavored yogurt sauce in which it's cooked. You'll need to soak the split peas for a couple of hours before you start cooking.

Cover the split peas with water in a bowl and set aside to soak for 2 hours. Drain the water and parboil in 2 cups (500 ml) fresh water in a saucepan over high heat for 8–10 minutes, or until just tender. Drain and set aside.

Heat the oil in a large wok over high heat. Once hot, fry the chicken, turning occasionally for 7–8 minutes, or until golden brown. Transfer the chicken to a plate using tongs or a slotted spoon.

Reduce the heat to medium, then add the onion, garlic, ginger, and chilies to the wok, and fry for 2–3 minutes, or until soft and fragrant. Stir in the yogurt, turmeric, 1 tablespoon salt (or to taste), and 1 teaspoon ground black pepper.

Return the chicken to the wok, along with the split peas, and cook, stirring occasionally, over low heat for 10–15 minutes, or until the chicken is cooked through and no longer pink inside when cut, and the split peas are soft. Stir in the tomatoes and cook for a further 2–3 minutes, or until the tomatoes soften.

Serve the morgh lawang on a large platter, garnished with the lime or lemon slices, red onion, and cilantro leaves.

GOSFAND LAWANG

گوشفند لونگ

½ cup (4 oz/113 g) yellow split peas
1 cup (250 ml) sunflower oil
1 large yellow onion, finely diced
3 garlic cloves, grated
Heaped 1 tablespoon grated fresh ginger
3 moderately hot fresh red chilies,
    thinly sliced, plus extra, halved
    lengthways, to serve
½ cup (4½ oz/130 g) plain yogurt
2 teaspoons ground turmeric
2¼ lb (1 kg) lamb shoulder,
    bone in, diced
2 large ripe tomatoes, finely diced
1 lime or lemon, thinly sliced
½ red onion, thinly sliced
2½ tablespoons fresh cilantro leaves
Salt and freshly ground black pepper

This lamb kebab dish is again called a lawang because of the yogurt sauce in which it develops its mouthwatering flavors. You'll need to soak the split peas for a couple of hours before you start cooking.

Cover the split peas with water in a bowl and set aside to soak for 2 hours. Drain the water from the split peas and parboil them in 2 cups (500 ml) fresh water in a saucepan over high heat for 8–10 minutes, or until just tender. Drain and set aside.

Heat the oil in a large wok over high heat and fry the yellow onion, garlic, ginger, and chili for 2 minutes, or until tender and fragrant. Stir in the yogurt, turmeric, 1 tablespoon salt (or to taste) and 1 teaspoon freshly ground black pepper to combine.

Reduce the heat to low-medium then add the lamb and split peas to the wok and cook for 30 minutes, or until the lamb is cooked through and tender when pierced, the split peas are soft, and the sauce has thickened. Stir in the tomatoes to combine and cook for a further 2–3 minutes, or until the tomato softens.

Serve straight from the wok, with the lime or lemon slices, red onion, cilantro, and extra chili alongside.

KARAYEE GOSFAND

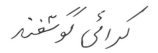

⅓ cup (80 ml) sunflower oil
6¾ lb (3 kg) lamb backstrap or loin
  fillet, cut into large strips
2½ tablespoons coriander seeds, crushed
  in a spice grinder or mortar and pestle
2½ tablespoons dried red pepper flakes
Heaped 1 tablespoon ground cumin
Heaped 1 tablespoon ground ginger
2½ tablespoons chaar masalah (see page 21)
5 ripe tomatoes, puréed in a blender
¼ cup (2½ oz/70 g) plain yogurt
1 large yellow onion, thinly sliced
2 moderately hot fresh red chilies,
  thinly sliced
2½ tablespoons fresh cilantro leaves,
  coarsely chopped
2 scallions, thinly sliced
Naan flatbread (see page 82), to serve
Salt and freshly ground black pepper

This dish combines lamb with several delicate spices, including the chaar masalah blend (see page 21), for the perfect balance of flavors. It is traditionally made in a karayee—a large, shallow, heavy-based pan, like that used to make tokhme banjanromi (see page 65). Because a karayee allows liquid to evaporate quickly while cooking, the result is meat that is deliciously tender, but not swimming in sauce, and infused with the flavors of the vegetables and spices with which it's cooked.

Traditionally, the hot karayee would be placed at the center of the dining table so people can help themselves to the lamb and vegetables, which are almost always enjoyed with hot naan flatbread, either homemade or store-bought.

Heat the oil in a large karayee, or shallow, heavy-based frying pan over high heat. Once hot, carefully add the lamb and fry, turning occasionally, for 10–15 minutes, or until browned. Reduce the heat to medium, then add the spices, 1 tablespoon salt (or to taste), and 1 tablespoon ground black pepper. Mix, then fry for 2–3 minutes, or until fragrant.

Stir in the tomatoes and yogurt to combine, bring to a boil, then reduce the heat to low and simmer, stirring occasionally, for 20–25 minutes, or until the meat is cooked through and tender when pierced.

Add the onion and fresh chili, stir to combine, and cook for another 2–3 minutes, or until they just soften. Serve hot on a large serving platter, garnished with cilantro and scallions, and with naan flatbread on the side.

CHAPLI KEBAB

چپلی کباب

1 small yellow onion, coarsely chopped
1 moderately hot fresh red chili, coarsely chopped, plus extra, halved lengthways, to serve
1 small handful fresh cilantro, coarsely chopped, plus extra leaves to serve
1 garlic clove, coarsely chopped
1 lb 2 oz (500 g) ground beef
1 teaspoon coriander seeds, crushed in a spice grinder or mortar and pestle
Heaped 1 tablespoon dried red pepper flakes
2½ tablespoons all-purpose flour
8 scallions, thinly sliced
1 large egg
1 cup (250 ml) sunflower oil
Naan flatbread (see page 82), thinly sliced red onion, chutney sabz (see page 86) and chutney morcheh sorkh (see page 87), to serve
Salt and freshly ground black pepper

These are flavor-packed thin beef or lamb patties full of fresh herbs and spices. In Afghanistan, they are a popular street food. My mother recalls that, when she was a child, on long family road trips, they would make pit stops at chapli kebab stalls on the roadside. She remembers the redness of the patties, since they were usually packed with chili and served wrapped in hot tandoori-baked naans with fresh vegetables and some tangy chutney on top.

◆

Process the yellow onion, fresh chili, cilantro, and garlic in a food processor until finely chopped. Place the ground beef in a medium bowl and add the blended ingredients, along with the spices, flour, scallions, egg, 2 teaspoons salt, and 1 teaspoon freshly ground black pepper. Mix thoroughly with your hands for 5 minutes, or until everything is well combined and the texture is slightly sticky. Cover the bowl with plastic wrap and refrigerate for 30 minutes to chill.

Divide the meat mixture into 8 equal portions and roll each into a ball between your palms. Lightly grease your hands with oil, then flatten the balls on a nonstick baking tray into patties roughly 4 in (10 cm) in diameter and ½ in (1 cm) thick.

Add the oil to a large frying pan over high heat. When it reaches 350°F (180°C) on an oil thermometer, add the patties to the pan in batches and fry at this temperature, turning occasionally, for 2–3 minutes, so they half-cook and retain their shape. Transfer the patties to a plate lined with paper towels and repeat this high-temperature frying until all the patties are half-cooked. Reduce the heat to low and fry the patties again in batches for 5 minutes each side, or until they are crisp and deep golden brown. Transfer to a plate lined with paper towels to drain the excess oil.

To serve, wrap the chapli kebabs in large pieces of Afghan flatbread, then top with chutney, onion slices, extra chili, and cilantro to taste.

NAAN FLATBREAD

ﻧﺎن

This recipe is for the bread that is traditionally eaten alongside almost any Afghan meal. Although naan would usually be bought from the local naanwahi (bakery), my mother remembers occasions as a child when naan was made at home; a gentle, warm, and inviting aroma filling the house as they cooked. Once she had met my father, my mother recalls that his mother was known far and wide for the especially delicious naan she would bake.

4¾ cups (1 lb 5 oz/600 g) all-purpose flour, plus more for dusting
2 teaspoons instant yeast
1½ cups (375 ml) lukewarm water
2½ tablespoons plain yogurt
2½ tablespoons sunflower oil, plus more for greasing
Salt

Place the flour, yeast, and 2 teaspoons salt in a medium bowl and whisk to combine. In a separate bowl, whisk the remaining ingredients to combine.

Create a well in the center of the dry ingredients, then slowly add the wet ingredients to the well, mixing to combine with your hands until a soft, slightly sticky dough forms.

Lightly dust a work surface with flour and knead the dough for 5 minutes, or until it is no longer sticky, and is soft and elastic.

Place the dough in a lightly greased bowl and cover with a tea towel. Set aside in a warm place, or at least at room temperature, for 40 minutes–1 hour, or until the dough has doubled in size.

Preheat the oven to 400°F (200°C) and line two baking pans with parchment paper. Divide the dough in half and spread one half into each baking pan with your hands, so that it fills the entire pan and is evenly spread. Place the pans in the oven and bake for 15 minutes, or until the naans are golden brown and baked through.

Naan flatbread is best enjoyed freshly baked and hot with any meal, but it will keep well in an airtight container for one day.

NAAN-E ROGHANI

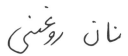

½ cup (125 ml) sunflower oil,
  plus 2 teaspoons extra
1½ cups (375 ml) lukewarm water
2 teaspoons sugar
2 teaspoons instant yeast
6 cups (1 lb 10½ oz/750 g) all-purpose
  flour, plus extra for dusting
¼ cup (60 ml) milk
1 teaspoon nigella seeds
1 teaspoon white sesame seeds
Salt

This is very similar to naan flatbread (opposite), but differs in that it has a softer pillow-like texture because of the extra oil added to it. Usually brushed with milk and then studded with nigella and sesame seeds, this naan bread is hard to resist. It is usually eaten at breakfast time, with some slightly sweetened green or black tea, or shir chai (see page 218).

In a large bowl, whisk the oil, water, sugar, yeast, and 4 teaspoons salt. Cover and set aside in a warm place or at least room temperature, for about 15 minutes, or until frothy.

Place the flour in a separate large bowl. Make a well in the center then slowly pour in the yeast mixture, mixing with your hands to combine well. The dough that forms should be soft and sticky. Add the extra 2 teaspoons of oil to help release the sticky dough from the bowl.

Turn out the dough onto a work surface lightly dusted with flour. Knead for 5 minutes, or until soft and elastic. Place the dough in a lightly greased bowl, cover with plastic wrap, and place a tea towel over the top. Set aside in a warm place to rest for 1½–2 hours, or until roughly doubled in size. Meanwhile, preheat the oven to 350°F (180°C) and line two baking pans with parchment paper.

Divide the dough into 4 equal portions. Place them on the pans, and flatten and spread each portion into rounds with your hands, ensuring they are relatively even in thickness. Push your fingertips into each round to create indentations, then brush with milk and sprinkle with the nigella and sesame seeds.

Bake for 15–20 minutes, or until the naans are golden brown and cooked through. Serve hot with shir chai for breakfast.

SALAATEH AFGHANI

سلاطه افغانی

1 large red onion, halved and
  thinly sliced
2 large tomatoes, finely diced
2 Persian or Lebanese cucumbers,
  finely diced
8-10 radishes, trimmed, thinly sliced,
  and quartered
1 large handful fresh cilantro leaves,
  coarsely chopped
1 large handful fresh mint leaves,
  coarsely chopped
1 fresh long green chili, thinly sliced
2 heads baby romaine lettuce,
  finely chopped
4 scallions, thinly sliced
2 limes, halved and juiced, plus extra
  wedges to serve
Salt

Seasonal vegetables nearly always accompany Afghan meals. In his garden, my grandfather grew tomatoes, cucumbers, citrus fruits, and herbs, which would be picked fresh and then finely chopped to make delicate-looking salads. Another favorite is radish, popular for its semi-bitter crunch, which complements many of the flavors infused into Afghan cooking.

Place all the ingredients, except the lime juice and salt, in a large bowl and toss to combine. In a small bowl, mix the lime juice with 1 teaspoon salt (or to taste), then drizzle over the salad and serve with extra lime wedges, alongside any Afghan meal.

CHUTNEY SABZ

چتنی شبز

Afghan meals are seldom complete without an assortment of fresh vegetables and relishes, such as chutney sabz.

A refreshing and zesty burst of herbs and acid, chutney sabz is the perfect accompaniment to any Afghan meal. Versatile and flavor-rich, this green chutney can be enjoyed alongside many dishes, including tokhme banjanromi (see page 65) at breakfast, with rice and curries, or simply as a dip for fresh naan breads (see pages 82 and 83).

1 large handful mint leaves
1 large handful fresh cilantro leaves and stems
2 fresh long green chilies, coarsely chopped
1 garlic clove, coarsely chopped
2 limes, juiced
2½ tablespoons white vinegar
Salt

Wash the herbs and put into a food processor, along with the chili and garlic. Process to a coarse paste.

Add the lime juice, vinegar, 2½ tablespoons cold water, and 1 teaspoon salt, then pulse to just combine.

This chutney is best enjoyed on the day it's made, while the fresh herbs maintain their vibrant green color. It can be kept in a sealed jar in the refrigerator for 3–4 days, but the color will slowly begin to darken.

CHUTNEY MORCHEH SORKH

3¼ cups (1 lb 2 oz/500 g) coarsely
  chopped red bell peppers
7 oz (200 g) moderately hot fresh red
  chilies, coarsely chopped
3 garlic cloves, coarsely chopped
1 teaspoon white sugar
1 teaspoon sweet paprika
¼ cup (60 ml) white wine vinegar
Salt

This chutney has a red-chili base from the inclusion of sweet red peppers and fresh red chilies. It can be made as hot or mild as you like, but is usually hotter than chutney sabz (see opposite). Chutney morcheh sorkh takes a bit more time to make than its green counterpart, but it keeps for longer because it has been cooked.

This chutney can be enjoyed alongside almost any Afghan meal, but especially as an accompaniment to the many kebabs and naan breads in this chapter.

Put the bell peppers, chilies, and 1 cup (250 ml) water into a small saucepan over high heat. Bring to a boil, then reduce the heat to low, cover with a lid, and cook slowly for 15–20 minutes, or until the vegetables soften. Add the garlic to the pan and cook for another 15 minutes, or until the ingredients are completely soft and the flavors are combined. Set aside to cool completely.

Once cooled, transfer the pepper mixture to a food processor and blend until puréed. Strain through a fine sieve into a bowl, then return the strained purée to the saucepan over medium-high heat. Add the sugar, paprika, vinegar, and 1 teaspoon salt, and stir to combine. Bring to a boil, then reduce the heat to low, cover with a lid to prevent splatter, and simmer for 10 minutes, or until slightly thickened.

Set aside to cool completely before serving. Chutney morcheh sorkh can be stored in a sterilized jar in the fridge for up to 2 weeks.

From left to right:
Chutney morcheh
sorkh (page 87);
Chutney sabz (page 86)

HALWAH-EH ARD-EH SUJI

This traditional sweet is usually made from three basic ingredients: flour, oil, and sugar, but different spices and nuts can be added to create variations. The ingredients that constitute halwah might be simple, but the way it's made requires technique—it involves lots of stirring! When made by an experienced hand, halwah is not heavy and greasy, but takes on an almost melt-in-the-mouth texture.

Apart from being a favorite sweet enjoyed particularly at breakfast, or with chai and naan bread at any time of the day, halwah is an auspicious dish in Afghan tradition. It is made as a kind of nazr, or offering, when people pass away, and is associated with the concept of blessings.

When my grandmother Hamida passed away, family and friends gathered to send their prayers for, and thoughts to, the young family left behind. The sweetness of halwah is symbolic at this time as comfort and recognition of a tragic yet inevitable part of life—loss.

This specific halwah, with semolina and almonds, is traditionally made to commemorate a loved one's passing.

2⅓ cups (15½ oz/440 g) sugar
6 cups (1.5 liters) boiling water, plus 1 cup (250 ml) extra
2 teaspoons saffron threads
1 teaspoon ground cardamom
2½ tablespoons slivered almonds
1½ cups (375 ml) sunflower oil
2 cups (13 oz/360 g) coarse semolina
2½ tablespoons slivered pistachios
Salt

Stir the sugar and boiling water in a small saucepan to dissolve the sugar. Place over high heat and bring to a boil. Stir the saffron, cardamom, almonds, and a pinch of salt into the syrup, then remove the pan from the heat.

Heat the oil in a medium heavy-based saucepan over high heat for 1 minute. Reduce the heat to medium, then add the semolina and stir to combine. Increase the heat to high again and keep stirring for 10 minutes; it's important to continue stirring to avoid the semolina burning or forming a crust at the bottom of the pan. At about the 5-minute mark, the semolina will begin to bubble, and after 10 minutes, you should be able to smell the semolina toasting.

Remove the saucepan from the heat and ladle the syrup (including the almonds) over the semolina, mixing continuously, until all the syrup has been added. Add the extra 1 cup (250 ml) boiling water and mix well to combine.

Place the pan over very low heat, cover with a lid, and gently cook, without stirring, for 5–6 minutes, or until the syrup starts to be absorbed. Turn off the heat and stir the halwah, then replace the lid and set aside for 10 minutes, or until the syrup has been completely absorbed and the halwah has expanded in size.

While it's still hot, sprinkle the halwah with slivered pistachios and serve.

HALWAH-EH ARD

حلواۀ آرد

This halwah is made with flour, and is usually served with naan bread and tea. An elder from my mother's time in Afghanistan would say that the special sweet aroma that fills the air when the flour first hits the hot oil in the pot rises up to the highest heavens, where even angels can smell the perfume.

2⅓ cups (15½ oz/440 g) sugar
5¼ cups (1.25 liters) boiling water,
  plus 1 cup (250 ml) extra
2 teaspoons ground cardamom
1½ cups (375 ml) sunflower oil
2½ cups (10½ oz/300 g) all-purpose flour
Edible rose petals, to serve
Salt

Combine the sugar and boiling water in a small saucepan and stir to dissolve the sugar. Place the pan over high heat and bring to a boil. Stir the cardamom and a pinch of salt into the syrup, then remove the pan from the heat.

Heat the oil in a medium heavy-based saucepan over medium heat until hot, but not smoking. Add the flour and mix continuously until the flour turns a deep brown color, then reduce the heat to low. Add the syrup, one ladle at a time, taking care to avoid splattering, and stirring continuously until all the syrup is absorbed.

By this point, the halwah should be forming and coming away from the sides of the pan rather than sticking. Add the extra 1 cup (250 ml) boiling water and keep stirring for 5 minutes, or until it is completely absorbed. At this stage, the halwah should have released some of its oil and be quite glossy.

Turn off the heat, cover the saucepan with a lid, and set aside to rest for at least 10 minutes before serving. In these final few minutes, the heat trapped in the bottom of the pan will continue to gently cook the halwah. Serve hot, sprinkled with edible rose petals.

From top:
Halwah-eh ard (page 91);
Halwah-eh ard-eh suji (page 90);
Halwah-eh kadoo (page 95)

HALWAH-EH KADOO

حلوا کدو

This halwah is made using pumpkin instead of flour. The result is sticky and delicious.

½ cup (125 ml) sunflower oil
2¼ lb (1 kg) pumpkin or winter squash, such as hubbard or Queensland blue, peeled, seeded, and grated
1 loosely packed cup (5¼ oz/150 g) light brown sugar
1 teaspoon ground cardamom
½ cup (2 oz/60 g) coarsely chopped walnuts
Slivered pistachios, to serve

Heat the oil in a heavy-based saucepan over medium heat for about 1 minute. Add the pumpkin and sugar, increase the heat to high, and stir to combine. Continue to stir for about 10 minutes, or until the pumpkin releases moisture; the liquid will help to further cook and soften the pumpkin.

Continue to mix for 15 minutes, to ensure the base doesn't burn and form a crust, or until the liquid in the halwah has reduced and the oil is released. It should be glossy and a deep rich brown color. Add the cardamom and walnuts to the halwah and mix to combine. Turn off the heat, cover the pan with a lid, and set aside to gently steam for another 5–10 minutes. Serve hot, sprinkled with slivered pistachios.

Chapter 3

The Dissipation
of a Dream

فصل سّوم

FINAL FOOTSTEPS ON
ANCIENT LANDS

فصل شُشوم

"The flames that devoured the houses
Were red
And left ashes

The blood they shed and poured
On the calendar of the year
Are still red

The autumn leaves
The dismal sunset
Were red
Red

Even the color of my nightmares
Are all red
Red, red"

Laila Sarahat Rushani, mid-twentieth-century Afghan poet

For centuries, the stability of the region now known as Afghanistan arose from a delicate, but well understood and adhered to, tripartite agreement between various tribes, the monarchy, and religious leaders. Each branch of this agreement seemed to balance the others in an overall equilibrium of sorts and, as long as the rights and voices of each were recognized, no single facet could overpower the others to solely rule. During the nineteenth and early twentieth centuries, as Afghanistan became a nation state, this was the balance of power my great-grandparents and grandparents were born into.

But, in the middle of the twentieth century, as my mother entered her adult years, times were changing. The validity of each branch of the agreement was being tested. Tribal ways seemed ossified, the need for a monarchy was being challenged, and religious leaders were, in some instances, becoming more vocal and dogmatic in response to the changing nature of the world around them.

It is not difficult to see how the tripartite that had previously provided a notion of stability and understanding among what had always been an unlikely amalgam of numerous ethno-linguistic tribes, no longer adequately captured the hopes of many Afghan people. In some cases it actively hindered them. The most conspicuously overlooked aspirations were those of women, who held little sway in established religious, political, or tribal codes, and, more generally, anyone who had not been born into one of the well-to-do families that benefitted most from the hierarchical and genealogical social structures that governed everyday life.

The need for change was palpable, but, instead of Afghanistan's own intellectual, political, literary and poetic vanguard coaxing the nation into the next iteration of itself, it would be the imported ideology of Soviet-inspired communism—and the increasingly severe version of Islam this energized in response—that would radically deplete the ancient aura of the nation, and the lives of the people who called it home.

The trajectory of my family's story changed drastically during the years after 1979. For the nation as a whole it was an era of change—one that would seriously endanger the people's capacity to hope and dream unencumbered, sending the traditional rhythm of the country into exile.

The foreboding rise of a president

As his reign matured, the king, Zahir Shah, recognized the need for the nation's evolution. He had managed to steer Afghanistan through World War II as a neutral country with its borders still intact and, afterwards, embarked on a mission to democratize the nation. He founded the first modern university in the country, brought in foreign advisers, and fostered diplomatic and commercial relations with Europe and with both sides of the Cold War—the United States and Soviet Russia. This opening up of the nation contributed to expanding the people's horizons even further. By the 1960s and 70s, many young Afghans had been educated to university level, either at home or overseas in the United States, Soviet Russia or Europe. They had seen for themselves the gap between the industrialized world and their own reality, and were looking for greater transformations at home.

The pinnacle of the democratization came with the constitution of 1964 that my great-uncle Shamsuddin Majrooh helped to draft, and which was the king's blueprint for transformation. It heralded an era of rights to establish political parties, the election of a new parliamentary assembly, civil rights, women's rights, and universal suffrage. In what would prove to be a critical moment in the future trajectory of the nation, in a bid to guard against nepotism, it included a clause that disallowed family members of the king from holding official roles. In anticipation, the king's cousin, Daoud Khan, who had served as

prime minister since 1953, stepped down in 1963 before the implementation of the constitution that would have forced his resignation.

In the first of many tragic and ironic twists, it was precisely these attempts at reform that would sear the initial chaotic schism into the nation's modern history. And this original wound was not inflicted by one of the many foreign interests who would soon attempt to mold the nation into a shape that would best guarantee their own success, but by its own leaders— men of varying religious and political convictions, but whose common desire for power was their most defining, and destructive, trait.

The first to strike a blow was the former prime minister. Daoud Khan's personal ambitions had not been quelled by his resignation of his official position— besides, the constitution that precluded him from holding office in the name of democratic liberalism would soon be rendered inconsequential. Restless and impatient with the pace of change, in 1973 Daoud Khan instigated a coup d'état in which he deposed his cousin from the throne and seized power. He then broke from tradition and, instead of taking the title of shah, he declared the nation a republic and himself president. He began his office with a similar agenda to that which he had pushed as prime minister, with policies that were modernist, nationalist, and also Soviet-aligned. It was, in fact, with communist support that he had achieved his coup.

طاهر شاه، داود خان، شمس الدين مجروح و دوسرون

King Zahir Shah (first from left), Shamsuddin Majrooh (middle), and Daoud Khan (furthest right)

Daoud Khan had brought to an end the relatively stable rule of Zahir Shah. The deposed king would spend most of his remaining years in exile in Italy. It was the end of the monarchy in Afghanistan. The coup was met with little opposition by the Afghan people. For one, it was a bloodless takeover and, importantly, despite the intent of the 1964 constitution to preclude nepotism and move towards democratization, many still regarded the existence of the monarchy as a symbol of an outmoded, authoritarian way of governing. In such a climate, Daoud Khan's newly re-publicized nation was heralded by many Afghans as revolutionary and an opportunity to erase the elitism that excluded so many. He was offering something that was simultaneously different and familiar: as a member of the respected and dynastic family that had ruled for centuries, he was known and trusted; and his dubious rise to power could be overlooked by those who were eager to proceed with the transformations he was promising.

During this time, by late 1974, my mother and father, Zelmai, were married. They had been known to one another through family circles—my mother and father's families were both from the Pashtun province of Laghman. My two grandfathers had trained together in military school, served at the same time, and held one another in high regard. The impending marriage was seen as symbolic not only of their union, but of the joining of these two Laghman families.

My mother recalls her suitor as a handsome, clever, well-dressed law graduate from the University of Kabul. My mother was herself beautiful and driven, and in addition to the love of cooking instilled in her by her mother and grandmother, she thrived in her role as a teacher at a primary school called Koteh Sangi. Like her own mother, her passion was for literature. This was a couple welded together by intellect, friendship and love. Their wedding took place at the trendy Bagh-e Bala in Kabul, the summer palace built in 1893 by the Emir Abdur Rahman Khan, who died there in 1901. By the 1960s it had been transformed into a lavish restaurant and reception center. At my parents' wedding, guests feasted on a banquet that included ashak and mantu dumplings, three different types of palaw, lamb kebab on the spit, piles of traditional wedding desserts and various celebratory pastries, cakes and traditional custards.

Soon after my parents were married, my father began his job as a customs official at Kabul airport—a respectable position for a young man who was widely admired and seen to be going places. He was the eldest son in a family of military men, and this brought with it respect and expectation in equal measure. His father, Amin Khan, was working on high-level military infrastructure projects at a time when the nation's roads, airports and other infrastructure were being heavily developed—mostly with money pouring in from both America and Soviet Russia, placing Afghanistan in the middle as a Cold War pawn. In what would soon prove a dangerous fuse to be lighting, President Daoud Khan was quoted saying he was "happiest when lighting his American cigarettes with Soviet matches." Indeed, the funds my grandfather assigned to build the airports were American dollars, while the roads to them were paved with Soviet cement.

By the time my father was a teenager, his father had taken a second wife. This was then a widely accepted practice, in keeping with tribal codes and religious norms—but one which often relegated the first wife and her children to a lesser status. For my paternal grandmother, Bibi Mariam, my father and his younger brother, my uncle Baryalai, this led to years of isolation and hardship. Despite her suffering, my grandmother was a talented, kind, and resilient spirit—from a family of people who received and passed on wisdom—and she would spend her time teaching other women how to read or sew beautiful quilts.

As soon as my father had the means, Bibi Mariam came to live with him and my mother. While my parents worked, she spent her final days lovingly looking after her first grandchild—the only grandchild she would meet—my sister Fatema, who was born in 1976. In 1979 my grandmother died of cancer. She had endured a life of tragedy, but, in some consolation for my father when he honors her memory, it had ended in a place of love.

Fatema spent her childhood years spoiled not only by Bibi Mariam, but by extended family from both sides. She remembers birthday parties with cakes layered high, and celebrating Eid with tables full of sweets, including traditional cookies pasted onto festive-colored sheets of paper. In many ways her childhood was idyllic—she would spend afternoons after school with our mother, eating at various kebab shops, buying sweets from street vendors' carts, or shopping for the latest denims and dresses in the trendy boutiques that dotted the streets of Kabul. Together, they would catch the tram between home and Koteh Sangi school, where Fatema would eagerly accompany my mother to her classes.

While Daoud Khan's reign during this time also marked the beginning of the unexplained disappearances and murders of those perceived as agitators, for the most part, life for my family and for many others like ours, carried on as usual. However, the instances of visible violence and acts of authoritarianism that occasionally seeped into public awareness were clues to a deeper decay. The foundations of the nation were being undermined and larger cracks began to appear. As a Pashtun loyalist, Daoud Khan had alienated many of the country's non-Pashtun ethnic groups, who were worried they might be sidelined by his policies. During the monarchy, most Afghans, regardless of ethnicity—whether that be Pashtun, Tajik, Hazara, or Uzbek—viewed the royal family as not favoring any particular ethnic group or tribe. Loyalty of subjects to the royal family had been more important than any particular ethnicity. Furthermore, although throughout his decade as prime minister and upon first becoming president, Daoud Khan had been heavily Soviet aligned, later in his presidency he began to turn away from increasingly heavy-handed, controlling, and

conditional Soviet support. By 1977 he had pivoted the country towards Egypt, Saudi Arabia, and the United States—which irked and heightened tensions with the Soviet leader, Leonid Brezhnev, during this Cold War era. Meanwhile, a growing Islamist movement was stirring, and rallying against the tendency towards liberalization, socialism, and Western-alignment that the government was pursuing. Cognisant of its existence and its potential to undermine the state, Daoud Khan would imprison or exile many of the leaders of this movement. But, most fatefully, the increasingly powerful communist factions of Afghanistan's parliament—the Parchamis and Khalqis of the People's Democratic Party of Afghanistan (PDPA)—who had helped him rise to power, were beginning to turn against him.

In this tense environment, a prominent PDPA member, Mir Akbar Khyber, was assassinated. The funeral was used as a rally for the communists who blamed the government for his murder—a charge the government always denied. Nevertheless, PDPA leaders were using openly anti-state rhetoric and convinced other members that they would be targeted for execution next. Daoud Khan, true to his autocratic nature, responded by promptly arresting the PDPA leaders, including its three most prominent members, Nur Muhammad Taraki, Hafizullah Amin, and Babrak Karmal. This was enough to trigger the PDPA's long-planned takeover of the country, with the blessing of the Soviet Politburo, which had ideological aspirations to transform Afghanistan into a communist satellite state.

Life in a communist revolution

While he was under house arrest, Hafizullah Amin orchestrated a coup that would forever change the face of the nation. On April 27, 1978 the Saur Revolution was set in motion. In a blood-filled and endlessly tragic day and night in the nation's history, President Daoud Khan and sixteen members of his family were killed in the Arg, the royal palace in Kabul. Ironically, he was gunned down by the state-of-the-art Afghan Air Force he had received Soviet help to develop.

My mother and father had bought a beautiful house in the Kabul suburb of Karteh Seh, not far from the Arg. On the afternoon of the palace siege, my mother remembers being on the front veranda and hearing gunshots in the distance and the intimidating growl of Soviet fighter jets as they streaked overhead towards the president's residence. When she switched on the radio, there was nothing but instrumental music to the tune of the national dance, the attan, playing aimlessly on repeat. She knew something had shifted, and that the nation was in deep trouble. Her hunch was confirmed later that evening, when Amin's voice crackled over the radio, conveying words to the effect that the Khalqis had taken control and, using the propagandist language of revolution, assured the people that the scourge of the monarchic elite had been finally eliminated and that power was now in the hands of the people.

Whatever Daoud Khan's faults, he was the last of the line of dynastic rulers of the nation. With his and his family's murder came the death of traditional Afghan statesmanship and autonomy in Afghan leadership. His shortcomings would soon seem inconsequential when compared to the chaos wreaked by an unfamiliar value system peddled by the new and deeply divided communist leaders of the nation— and the radicalized, and hitherto-unknown, version of Islam that was inflamed in response. In a fitting sign of the bloodshed to come, the black, red, and

green tricolor flag of Afghanistan—representing the past, the bloodshed that had achieved the nation's independence, and the hope for the future of the nation—was replaced with the solid red of Soviet regalia.

The first to take power as president was Taraki, with Amin as his deputy—both from the Khalqi faction of the PDPA. On October 30, 1978 *The Kabul Times* printed "The Biography of the Great Leader," written in the stilted (and also hitherto-unknown in Afghanistan) language of communist propaganda. It declared: "great leader … Comrade Noor Mohammad Taraki is a dear friend to all hard-working, honest, and patriotic compatriots. He is a just leader and teacher. He is highly cultured, modest, and compassionate." It was not only the language that Afghans would find unconvincing, but also the ideology of the party. The communist party was trying to instil a new value system in the Afghan people, based on the idea that tribe, faith, and kinship no longer mattered.

While the PDPA had correctly seized upon the idea that change was due, they had gone about it in an impatient, provocative, and reckless way, and ended up dependent on the same hierarchy and elitism they were purporting to eliminate. The main targets of the party would be: the educated, who were labeled in many instances as "agents of American imperialism"; the religious—ranging from religious leaders, to those who privately practiced tenets of their faith, such as fasting and praying, to those who were non-practicing but refused to label themselves as communist—all of whom were given the condescending label "ikhwan," inferring religious fanaticism; and the land-owners and traditional tribal elites, who were at first courted by Taraki and his party but were quickly labeled "feudals," "exploiters," or "enemies of the state." The initial veneer of unification and revolution steered by the "great leader" rapidly disintegrated to reveal the brutal truth of a bloody-minded purge.

One of the biggest failings of the new communist ideology—and most serious misjudgements of the mood of the people—was its land reform policy. The premise was that land should be redistributed from the land-owners—the bourgeoisie—into the hands of the peasant farmers who worked the land. By catalyzing this large but usually ignored portion of the population, Taraki and his party believed they could garner popular support. But the party leaders mistakenly assumed that material wealth was most important to the people. There were, in fact, deeper layers of conviction in Afghan culture, which had long been bound by codes of honor and personal conduct that were entrenched in notions of rightfulness, such as "amanat"—someone's rightful belonging—and "rohzi"—someone's rightful sustenance.

By asking peasants to take land that they did not see as rightfully their own, the communist leaders were asking them to partake in something alien and violating. Humiliated and made to take part in publicly held Soviet-style ceremonies, in which new deeds signed by Taraki reassigned parcels of land to the landless, many of the farmers refused to benefit and would secretly hand back the profits of the harvest. Not only were the land-reform decrees rejected by the spirit of the people, but they were also poorly and haphazardly organized and resulted in a significant reduction in agricultural production, which would strain the entire nation.

In Laghman my maternal grandfather, Abdul Ghafour Khan, owned ancestral lands upon which various strains of rice were cultivated. Amid chants of "death to the feudal elites," shouted by the urban communist loyalists who had ventured into the countryside to bring the revolution to the peasants, my grandfather took part in a ceremony in which he gave land deeds to each of the farmers who worked for him. His character and values had been forged during the blossoming of the intellectual and spiritual revolution of Afghanistan that took place earlier in the twentieth century, and he felt most deeply distraught, not by the loss of land, but by the disorientation caused by this unmodified importation of the codes of Soviet Russia.

These borrowed codes made little rational sense in Afghanistan—a country with an economy that was still not widely monetized and where the full extent of capitalism had not unfolded (a precursor that even Karl Marx noted as a condition necessary for a true proletarian revolution to take place). At the time of the communist revolution, land-owners were still heavily invested in the wellbeing of their communities—profits generally remained in the area and land-owners had guesthouses where tenant farmers, allies, friends, kin, and travelers were fed and sheltered.

In 1980, a month or so after my sister Zelaikhah was born, my grandfather passed away at the age of 59. My mother thinks his heart was partially broken by the grief of witnessing the chaos injected into Afghanistan. He did not live to see his country liberated from the disorientating communist ideology, but he died a man of his nation, and was remembered as dignified and uncompromised. When he passed, the roses and lilacs he loved the most were in full bloom in his gardens.

The people's uprising and the arrival of the Soviets

The rejection of communism by most people in Afghanistan—even the vast swathes who were usually apolitical—arose from the view that the government was overreaching into traditionally private matters. The rural opposition to land reform and other hastily applied PDPA decrees—including mixing genders in ways too liberal and too fast for many Afghans, and the steadily intensifying vilification of religion—was met by the communist regime with increased violence. Large-scale disappearances and indiscriminate killings perpetrated by the government were now in full swing. By 1979, outside urban areas, most of the country was beginning to revolt against the regime. In March of the same year an insurrection took place in Herat, when both the people and mutineering army troops turned against the government. Taraki asked for help from the Soviet regime to suppress the uprising; however, worried about becoming embroiled in Afghanistan's unrest, it refused to send ground troops. The Afghan regime eventually suppressed the mutiny unaided, killing thousands of civilians by aerial bombardment and burying them in mass graves. Across the country, those who opposed the regime were kidnapped and executed, or disappeared forever. The nation's prisons brimmed full with unrepentant Afghans.

The widespread violence was compounded by internal divisions and warring egos within the party leadership. While Amin positioned himself as the loyal protégé of Taraki, he was in fact vying for power. Restless with ambition, and with animosity growing between "master" and "disciple," in early October of 1979, Amin maneuvered his own power base to eliminate Taraki. While publicly Amin declared that Taraki was gravely ill, in truth, Taraki's own guards had suffocated him to death on Amin's orders. It had only been about a year and a half since the Saur Revolution, but already long-brewing treachery and personal ambition were beginning to eclipse any communist pretence of service to the people.

The seizure of power by Amin was a bitter pill for the Soviet rulers. They had always backed Taraki and were alarmed by Amin's actions. They also felt they could not trust Amin, who seemed inclined to pivot the nation's foreign policy towards America. In December 1979 the Soviets finally sent in troops—a move they had previously resisted on several occasions. In a plot that involved KGB agents, poison at dinner, and aerial bombardments of the royal palace, a paltry matter of days after seizing leadership, Amin was killed by his own overlords on December 27, 1979. This time, it was the voice of Karmal—also a communist party member, but from the Parcham faction—that crackled over the airwaves of Radio Kabul, alerting the people that "the torture machine of Amin had been obliterated." Karmal had been parachuted into power by a Soviet regime worried about losing its grip on Afghanistan. The Soviet plan was to stay in Afghanistan for a short time only, to help to prop up and secure Karmal's leadership, but they were met with, and stunned by, the fierce resistance of the mujahideen—civilians who had been largely organized and galvanized into action in response to the widespread violence of the Saur Revolution. The Soviets became embroiled in an occupation that lasted almost a decade.

Almost immediately during this era of Soviet occupation, an atmosphere of suspicion and extreme censorship prevailed. For ordinary people, refusing to pledge allegiance to the communist party was an act of insubordination that was met with swift punishment. People became very careful of what was said and to whom, as informants were planted throughout society. Before the arrival of communism, my father felt as though his future was laid out before him. After the occupation, life prospects were drastically diminished. Corruption and incompetence became commonplace, as workers without necessary training or qualifications rocketed to positions of power simply by pledging allegiance to communism.

The first signs of manipulation came when my father was asked by his senior in the Customs Office to funnel money into the senior's account. Within a week of refusing to put his signature to the request, he was sent a letter relieving him of his duties. Over the coming months, it became increasingly difficult for him to find work; he had been blacklisted as non-compliant to the communist cause.

When he finally found another position it was far beneath his level of experience and standing, and with the same sinister undertones that were becoming widespread in the nation. It was a position in the Department of Finance, in a subdivision responsible for reassigning the goods repossessed from people who had been executed, disappeared, or who had fled the country in fear for their life. In this role, he was again asked to assign money to line the pockets of those in senior positions. Again, he refused. A few days later, a senior, known to be high in the communist ranks, came to visit the office under the pretence of checking on how the work was unfolding. When he had the chance, he quietly pulled my father aside and explained that he was not ideologically communist, but had publicly pledged allegiance in order to save his life. He told my father that he was there to warn him; there had been whispers labeling my father "ikhwan" for refusing to comply with state orders. It was only a matter of time before he would be killed. My father said his knees felt weak. At lunchtime he walked into his boss's office to let him know he was going home sick for the day. He never went back.

The exile of a culture

My sister Zahra had been born in 1981, and myself in 1985. Apart from Fatema, we were all born into a communist regime that, with each iteration of its leadership, seemed to become more brutal. By the time the Soviets were on Afghan soil, large numbers of civilians were being killed indiscriminately and scorched-earth policies and extensive depopulation were being carried out.

The situation was further exacerbated by the amplified international interference, with other nations using Afghanistan as a canvas to further their own aims. During the Cold War era America had an especially intense interest in ensuring the demise of the Soviet Union and was furthering its agenda via covert CIA operations, with extensive cooperation from Pakistan. This was not the first time Afghanistan had been squeezed in the middle of a superpower sandwich, but the players had shifted—from Tsarist Russia against the British Empire throughout the nineteenth century, to communist Russia against the successor to Western power, America, during the twentieth century.

But this time, in an increasingly globalized and militarized world, the consequences for Afghanistan would become progressively more dire. By the 1970s and 80s, Afghanistan was awash with funds and weapons from Iran, China, Europe, Saudi Arabia, and America. The country had been weaponized to the brim. And, while this meant the mujahideen were well placed to defeat the Russians, it also meant increasingly destructive warfare, including the planting of hundreds of thousands of landmines, many of which lie undetonated to this day. In addition, incentivized by the stream of money coming in from countries such as Saudi Arabia, and in an environment where the culture's rich historical amalgam of identities had been reduced to the simple binary of communist against Muslim, an increasingly fanatical version of Islam was brewing for the first time in Afghanistan's history. The mujahideen resistance—at first the struggle of ordinary Afghans who had been forsaken by their own leaders and were fighting for their country and their kin—had warped into different factions of Islamist movements, among the most prominent being Gulbuddin Hekmatyar's Hizb-i Islami and Burhanuddin Rabbani's Jamiat-i Islami. These were precursors to the Taliban, funded by a global coalition. Many operated from across the border in Pakistan, where their ideologies were not opposed by the government, and all attempted to prove their legitimacy by using increasingly severe interpretations of Islam as a measure of their worthiness to lead.

Soviet war in Afghanistan he ran a small journalistic center called the Afghan Information Center. In a country flooded with both communist and Islamist propaganda, news sources from all over the world would come to Bahaouddin Majrooh for reliable and neutral information.

In a 1979 paper titled "Afghan intellectuals in exile: philosophical and psychological dimensions," he reported that one of the most dramatic aspects of the Soviet invasion was its rapid creation of what was, at the time, the largest population of refugees in the world—1.5 million internally displaced, 5 million in neighboring countries, and thousands more throughout the world. During this time, almost half the Afghan population of 16 million was living in exile.

By February 1989, defeated and depleted and with the Soviet Union on the brink of collapse, the Russians had left Afghanistan. The official estimate is that over one million civilians had been killed in under a decade—not soldiers or political agitators, but ordinary people. And, of those who survived, many had left the country.

My mother's cousin, Bahaouddin Majrooh, had closely monitored the impact of the war in Afghanistan. The son of my great-uncle, Shamsuddin Majrooh, was a polyglot—fluent in Pashtu, Farsi, English, French, and German—a philosopher, poet, journalist, provincial governor, and diplomat during the time of the last king, Zahir Shah, and former dean of the literature faculty at Kabul University. During the

The implications for the culture of the nation were profound. Bahaouddin Majrooh correctly observed that something deeper preceded and, in fact, enabled the physical displacement that was taking place. This was a psychological and spiritual exile that had been happening in the decades prior to the 1970s, when Afghan intellectuals were beginning to view the world through a lens of Western influence, in which their own ancient ways were dislocated, diluted, and demoted. The education system in Afghanistan had emerged in this way, with little relation to its proud local heritage. Instead of pressing forward with much-needed change and evolution in accordance with its own ancient and spiritual dimensions—Afghan classical intellectualism that had once merged traditional and

emerging ways—the nation pressed forward in the image of others. Now, the gap between the past and the present had become a wide gulf, and Afghanistan had become susceptible to imported ideologies—both communist and Islamist. Though espousing very different ideals, these were the same in the ways that counted: both claimed to be revolutionary, both took their inspiration from outside Afghanistan, and both were profoundly alienating and destructive to ordinary Afghans.

Coda: leaving ancient lands behind

Of the millions of families displaced, mine was one. Sensing that the situation was rapidly deteriorating, and with my father's life increasingly at risk, by 1985 my parents were preparing to take their final footsteps on their ancient homelands. They applied for travel papers into Pakistan under the guise of attending the wedding of a relative who lived across the border in Peshawar. At a time when movement was strictly inhibited and monitored, official papers were obtained by paying the right people. They placed the date of

the imaginary wedding on the eighth of the month. To leave, we needed to travel from Kabul to Jalalabad to Torkham, which was the gateway in the Khyber Pass between Afghanistan and Pakistan. It was generally men who were perceived as a threat and interrogated at checkpoints, so my father traveled separately, to avoid placing the entire family at risk.

Our plan was to meet him in Jalalabad, where the rest of the family had arrived a week earlier, and together travel the shorter distance to the Khyber Pass. On his solitary travels, my father had to pay someone to take the risk of driving him out of Kabul, where the chances of being stopped and interrogated—and then usually killed, imprisoned, or disappeared—by either communist or Islamist officials, were high. It had taken longer than anticipated for him to leave Kabul but, when he finally found a driver, in an unusual stroke of luck, their car evaded screening and my father was reunited with us in Jalalabad. But we had all been delayed by a day. On our travel papers the date of the wedding was altered to look like the ninth.

It was a desperate and risky, but unavoidable, move. By the time our crumpled paper was handed to the official in Torkham who was overseeing the flow of people across the border, it had obviously been tampered with. The border official looked at my dad and said, "It looks like you've missed the wedding." My father insisted we hadn't and that the wedding was later that very evening, the ninth. The official gave my father a knowing look and informed him that he could easily tell the paper had been altered. But, in yet another fateful turn of events, instead of detaining us, he said to my father: "Take your wife and your children and go. I know there's no wedding and that you have no intention of coming back. Don't come back, and may God help you along the way."

Decades earlier, my grandmother had warned that the nation's clouds would weep for its people. It must have felt that day had truly arrived for my parents, as we traversed under the shadow cast by the brooding skies of Afghanistan and crossed the border towards horizons unknown.

The recipes in this chapter reflect the reality faced by many who are displaced globally—that one of the first things to be undermined, corrupted, and dispirited is the natural and indigenous ways of the lands and its people. The rice recipes pay homage to lands seized and harvests never reaped, which plunged more and more ordinary Afghans into poverty and scarcity. Rice is a central feature of Afghan tradition and cuisine—intricate, fragrant, delicate, and jeweled, it non-verbally rebuts the censorship and obliteration of ancient cultural ways that the occupying forces of this era conspired to induce.

This chapter also includes dishes made to mark celebratory occasions, because even among chaos and high-level politicking, for many ordinary people the instinct is to continue with normal life for as long as possible. In this way, even during a communist takeover and the fomenting of depraved religious corruptions, my parents were married, had children, bought their first house, buried loved ones, and celebrated Eid and their children's birthdays. Despite the upheavals, food continued to play a central and comforting role in their lives and remained a potent way to connect to their memories of happier times, and to the traditional ways of old that had shaped them.

THE ART OF AFGHAN RICE

Rice is a staple of Afghan cuisine. Intricately flavored, beautifully garnished, and usually copiously piled onto large serving platters, rice is rarely eaten alone, but forms the centerpiece of most Afghan meals. Because of the level of detail and care taken in making most Afghan rice dishes, how well rice can be made is usually interpreted as a measure of the cook's overall talent and grasp of the cuisine. The type of rice prepared would traditionally depend on a person's prosperity or on the significance of the occasion—with the more time-consuming and expensive rice dishes, such as **kabuli palaw** (see page 113), considered a luxury reserved for special guests and events.

Afghan cuisine distinguishes its rice dishes by the technique used to cook the rice, which results in three categories: **palaw, challaw,** and **sholah.** Furthermore, within each category, there is an array of toppings that crown the pillowy piles of rice, as well as a variety of ingredients—such as vegetables, legumes, and meats—that are blended through the rice, creating a panoply of distinctive dishes.

Palaws are prepared using long-grain rice, and their hallmark is that the rice grains are elongated and separated, and infused with the flavors added during the cooking process. **Challaws** are like palaws in terms of the texture of the rice, but a challaw is a simpler, plain white rice dish to eat alongside a variety of vegetable or meat curries. **Sholahs,** on the other hand, are prepared using a medium-grain rice that is cooked in such a way as to make it sticky and soft. The rice is always rinsed before cooking to remove any contaminants, such as small pebbles, which may have not been removed in the production process, while for palaws and challaws, the rice is also pre-soaked for 2–3 hours before rinsing to remove excess starch and help the grains elongate.

Parts of Afghanistan, including my family's province of Laghman, are perfectly suited for rice growing. On his land, my grandfather, Abdul Ghafour Khan, grew multiple varieties of rice, including long grains called dara dooni, many varieties of sella rice, and medium grains, both white and red, used to make sticky rice dishes. During the harvest, rice would be collected by hand, dried, and then roasted in giant clay vats to separate the grains from their husks. It would then go through a hydro-powered wooden machine called a **pai kohb**, which had two large hammers that would simultaneously pound the rice grains to further separate the husks and to also elongate the grains.

The rice would be distributed around the country and some of it stored at home. My sister Fatema recalls, as a child, seeing large clay barrels, known as **kandoos**, over three times her height in the attic of the family's provincial home. These **kandoos** were used to store rice for years, keeping it clean and dry as it aged. It would be used for the preparation of feasts marking special occasions, such as weddings or other significant **mehmanis**. My mother remembers the earthy fragrance this rice released as it cooked.

The art of cooking rice was one of the first things my mother learned as a young adult, as she spent time in the kitchens absorbing the traditional techniques of Afghan cooking.

CHALLAW

2 cups (13 oz/370 g) sella basmati rice,
   soaked for 2-3 hours
1 teaspoon bruised green cardamom pods
1 teaspoon cumin seeds
½ cup (125 ml) sunflower oil
1½ cups (375 ml) hot water
Salt

Challaw is a plain white rice dish and, like palaw, it's made using long-grain rice. The grains in a perfect challaw are elongated and separate, and it traditionally accompanies sauce-based dishes, such as kofta challaw (see page 122) or the turnip and lamb curry called shalgham challaw (see page 130). Soak the rice for 2-3 hours or longer before preparing challaw.

Bring 8½ cups (2 liters) water to a boil in a large pot. Drain any excess water from the rice, rinse under cold running water until the water runs clear, then add to the boiling water with 1 tablespoon salt. Boil the rice for 5-6 minutes, or until parboiled and the grains seem to have doubled in length.

Drain the rice in a colander, discarding the water, and return the rice to the pot. Add the cumin, cardamom, and 1 tablespoon salt and, using a kafgeer or large, flat slotted spoon, mix gently to combine. Add the oil and hot water, and stir gently to coat the rice grains.

Cover with a lid and cook over high heat for 5-6 minutes, or until steam escapes from beneath the lid; this is a critical step in preparing the rice to avoid it overcooking and becoming gluggy. Once you see the steam, reduce the heat to low and cook for another 20 minutes. Serve with your favorite sauce-based dish.

KABULI PALAW

FOR THE PALAW
½ cup (125 ml) sunflower oil
2 medium yellow onions, finely diced
1 lb 2 oz (500 g) diced boneless lamb leg
3 cups (1 lb 5 oz/600 g) sella basmati
 rice, soaked for 2-3 hours
1 teaspoon ground cumin
1 teaspoon ground cardamom

FOR THE TOPPING
2 cups (500 ml) sunflower oil
2 medium carrots, trimmed, peeled, and
 cut into thin matchsticks
Heaped 1 cup (6 oz/170 g) raisins or
 golden raisins
Heaped 1 tablespoon slivered almonds
Heaped 1 tablespoon slivered pistachios
2 teaspoons white sugar
1 teaspoon ground cardamom
Salt

This beautiful and balanced rice is Afghanistan's national dish. In a time before the convenience of julienne slicers and store-bought peeled and slivered nuts, kabuli palaw was time-consuming and elaborate to prepare, and was reserved primarily for ceremonial events. These days, although it takes less time to make, it still commands reverence. The delicate blend of spices and a crowning glory of glistening carrots, raisins, and nuts gives kabuli palaw pride of place among Afghan rice dishes.

Pieces of lamb or chicken are usually buried beneath the rice, with the stock from the meat used to flavor it. If you prefer, you can leave out the meat and use vegetable stock instead. This version uses lamb, cooked to tenderness in a pressure cooker. The rice should be soaked for at least 2-3 hours beforehand.

◆

To prepare the palaw rice, add the oil and onion to a pressure cooker pan over high heat and fry for 5 minutes, or until golden brown. Add the lamb and stir occasionally for 5 minutes, or until the meat is browned and sealed. Add 4¼ cups (1 liter) hot water and a heaped 1 tablespoon salt, place the lid on the pressure cooker, and bring to high pressure. Cook at high pressure for 15 minutes, then carefully release the pressure to remove the lid. Using a slotted spoon, take out the meat (which should be lovely and tender) and set aside. Reserve the stock to flavor the rice.

Bring 10 cups (2.5 liters) water to a boil in a large pot. Meanwhile, drain excess water from the rice, add it to the boiling water with 1 tablespoon salt, and cook for 6-8 minutes, or until the rice is parboiled and the grains look like they have doubled in length.

Drain the rice in a colander and return to the pot. Pour the meat stock over the rice, then add the cumin, cardamom, and 1 tablespoon salt to the mixture. Using a large, flat slotted spoon, known to Afghans as a kafgeer, mix gently. With the kafgeer, create a well in the center of the rice and place the lamb in the well. Cover the meat with rice and place the lid on the pot. Cook over high heat until steam escapes from under the lid, then reduce the heat to very low and cook for 20 minutes.

For the topping, heat the oil in a frying pan over high heat until shimmering. Add the carrot and fry for 4-5 minutes, or until slightly softened. Remove with a slotted spoon and set aside in a bowl. Add the raisins to the oil and fry for 3 minutes, or until they are plump and float to the surface. Remove with a slotted spoon and add to the bowl with the carrot. Add the nuts, sugar, and cardamom to the bowl, and mix gently.

Using the kafgeer, layer the rice and lamb onto a large serving platter, creating a heap. Liberally spoon over the topping and serve immediately.

NARENJ PALAW

Palaw rice (see page 113)
3 large navel or other oranges
1¾ cups (11½ oz/330 g) white sugar
Heaped 1 tablespoon slivered pistachios
Heaped 1 tablespoon slivered almonds
Salt

A delicate and fragrant rice dish topped with a mix of candied citrus peel and nuts, narenj palaw is popular in Afghan cuisine. Like kabuli palaw, it was often reserved for special occasions because of the delicacy of the ingredients and the time taken to prepare them.

In Afghanistan, the citrus peel comes from a fruit called narenj, which is a cross between an orange and a lemon, and more widely known as bitter orange. Here, where narenj isn't available, it can be substituted with the peel from any orange variety. The peel is blanched to extract any bitterness, and then soaked in syrup with the nuts to create a tangy, sweet, and aesthetically beautiful topping for the palaw.

To prepare the palaw rice base for this dish, follow the recipe for the palaw on page 113. Using a small sharp knife, cut the peel from the oranges in long strips and slice off any white pith. Layer two or three strips of rind on a cutting board and slice them diagonally into thin strips. Repeat until all the peel is cut.

To remove any bitterness in the rind, bring 4¼ cups (1 liter) cold water, ½ teaspoon salt, and the rind to a boil in a small saucepan. Add the rind and blanch by boiling for 2 minutes, then drain in a colander. Rinse under cold running water, drain again, and return the rind to the saucepan with another 4¼ cups (1 liter) of cold water and ½ teaspoon salt. Repeat the blanching process three more times, and set the rind aside.

In a small saucepan, stir the sugar into 1½ cups (375 ml) water until dissolved. Place the saucepan over high heat and cook without stirring for 6–8 minutes, or until the temperature reaches 200°F (100°C) on a candy thermometer and the syrup thickens slightly. Add the orange rind to the syrup and boil for 5 minutes, or until it is translucent and sweet. Add the pistachios and almonds, and stir gently to combine. Store the topping in the syrup until you're ready to use it.

To serve, gently layer the rice and lamb pieces onto the center of a large platter using a kafgeer, or large flat slotted spoon, creating a heap. Drain the narenj topping, discarding the syrup, and liberally spread over the rice to serve.

KICHIRI QOROOT

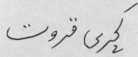

This sticky rice dish with mini kofta, and topped with a sizzling hot oil and yogurt mix. It is traditional winter fare, made with a tart reconstituted yogurt called qoroot, which can be something of an acquired taste, so it is often substituted with plain yogurt, as it is here.

4 large ripe tomatoes, quartered
1 garlic clove, coarsely chopped
½ cup (125 ml) sunflower oil
1 large yellow onion, finely diced
1 teaspoon white sugar
1 teaspoon curry powder
2½ tablespoons white vinegar
Heaped 1 tablespoon tomato paste
Salt and freshly ground black pepper

FOR THE MINI KOFTA
1 large yellow onion, coarsely chopped
1 long fresh red chili, coarsely chopped
Small handful fresh cilantro, leaves and
   stems coarsely chopped
1 garlic clove, coarsely chopped
9 oz (250 g) fatty ground lamb
9 oz (250 g) lean ground beef
1 teaspoon coriander seeds, ground with
   a spice grinder or mortar and pestle

FOR THE RICE
¼ cup (60 ml) sunflower oil
2 large yellow onions, finely diced
1 large ripe tomato
2¼ cups (15½ oz/440 g) medium-grain rice,
   such as Calrose, rinsed
1 cup (8 oz/225 g) mung beans

FOR THE TOPPINGS
3 cups (1 lb 11 oz/780 g) Greek-style
   yogurt
1 garlic clove, finely grated
½ cup (125 ml) sunflower oil
½ teaspoon ground turmeric
Red and green long fresh chili, thinly
   sliced, dried mint, and sweet paprika,
   to garnish

To make the kofta, finely blend the onion, chili, cilantro, and garlic in a food processor. Add ¼ cup (60 ml) water and blend again to form a fine paste. Place the lamb and beef in a large mixing bowl, add the blended paste with the ground coriander, 2 teaspoons salt, and 1 teaspoon freshly ground black pepper. Using your hands, mix to combine well for 5 minutes, or until the ingredients are fully incorporated and the mixture is slightly sticky. Shape teaspoonfuls of the kofta mixture into balls. Place them on a tray lined with parchment paper and refrigerate for at least 30 minutes to become slightly firm.

Meanwhile, finely blend the tomatoes and garlic in a food processor. Heat the oil in a large saucepan over high heat and fry the onion, stirring occasionally, for 5 minutes, or until golden brown. Add the blended tomatoes and garlic, and fry with the onion for 2 minutes, or until fragrant. Stir in the sugar, curry powder, vinegar, and 2 teaspoons salt (or to taste) and cook for another minute. Add the tomato paste and mix well to combine. Finally, add 3 cups (750 ml) water, bring the sauce to a boil, then reduce the heat to medium.

Add the kofta to the sauce, shaking the pan gently from side to side to make sure they are submerged. Increase the heat to high, bring to a boil, then reduce the heat to medium. Cover with a lid and simmer for 20–25 minutes, or until the sauce has reduced and thickened, and is rich in color.

While the sauce is cooking, make the rice. Add the oil to a large saucepan over high heat and fry the onions, stirring occasionally, for 5 minutes, until golden brown. Add the tomato and cook for a further 5 minutes, or until the tomato has softened. Add the rice and mung beans, with 6 cups (1.5 liters) water and 3 teaspoons salt. Bring to a boil, then reduce the heat to low and stir in another ½ cup (125 ml) water. Cover the pan and simmer for 40 minutes, or until the rice is cooked, soft, and sticky, but not mushy.

To make the toppings, whisk the yogurt, garlic, and ½ teaspoon salt in a small bowl to combine. This will be poured into the center of the kichiri qoroot. In a small saucepan, heat the oil over high heat to 325°F (170°C) on an oil thermometer. Remove from the heat and stir in the turmeric. Keep the oil hot.

Before serving, make sure the mini kofta and sauce are hot. Spoon the rice onto a large serving platter, making a well in the center. Nestle the mini kofta into the rice, drizzling some of the sauce over the rice as well. Garnish with the chili slices. Dot some yogurt dressing around the kofta and pour the rest into the well in the center of the rice. Sprinkle with the dried mint and paprika, then pour the hot turmeric oil over the yogurt to create a sizzling centerpiece, and serve.

Kichiri qoroot (page 116)

Sholeh Ghorbandi (page 120)

SHOLEH GHORBANDI

شوله غوربندی

Here is another warm, comfortingly sticky rice dish that is traditionally enjoyed in winter with a rich lamb curry called qormeh gosfand (see page 183).
This rice is named after the Ghorband district, northwest of Kabul, where the dish originates. Qormeh gosfand is served over the rice, infusing it with the rich flavors of the sauce. Prepare the curry before making the sholah rice, so it's all ready to serve at once.

½ cup (125 ml) sunflower oil
1 large yellow onion, finely diced
2 large tomatoes, coarsely diced
1 cup (8 oz/225 g) mung beans
2¼ cups (15½ oz/440 g) medium-grain rice,
*   such as Calrose, rinsed*
Qormeh gosfand (see page 183), to serve
Lime wedges and dill sprigs, to serve
Salt and and freshly ground black pepper

Heat the oil in a medium saucepan over high heat and fry the onion, stirring occasionally, for 5 minutes, or until golden brown.

Add the tomato, mung beans, 2 cups (500 ml) water, and 2½ tablespoons salt, bring to a boil, and cook for 15 minutes, or until the mung beans are parboiled (softened slightly, but not mushy).

Add the rice and another 6 cups (1.5 liters) water and boil for 5 minutes. Stir and cover with a lid, reduce the heat to medium-low, and simmer for 20 minutes, or until the rice has completely absorbed the liquid; at this stage, do not stir the rice or the grains will break and change the texture of the dish. Reduce the heat to very low and steam the rice for 10 minutes.

Carefully transfer the sholah rice to a large serving platter. Spoon hot qormeh gosfand on top, generously sprinkly with freshly ground black pepper, and serve immediately with lime wedges and dill sprigs.

SHOLEH GOSHTI

شوله گوشتی

1 lb 2 oz (500 g) diced boneless lamb leg
1 cup (250 ml) sunflower oil
2 large yellow onions, finely diced
3 large ripe tomatoes, diced
1 cup (8 oz/225 g) mung beans
2¼ cups (15½ oz/440 g) medium-grain rice,
  such as Calrose, rinsed
2 moderately hot fresh red chilies
2 teaspoons ground cumin
2 teaspoons coriander seeds, ground with
  a spice grinder or mortar and pestle
Small handful fresh dill sprigs,
  finely chopped
5¼ cups (1.25 liters) boiling water
Salt

For this sticky rice dish, the lamb is cooked with the rice, infusing it with the flavors of the meat. A hearty and filling dish, this is typical winter fare in Afghanistan, and is occasionally used as nazr—an offering shared with others to help fulfil a certain desire or prayer. In the southern provinces, it was also traditionally served to feed large numbers of guests at weddings.

Place the lamb in a pressure cooker pan with 3 cups (750 ml) water and a heaped 1 tablespoon salt, and seal it shut. Bring the cooker to high pressure over high heat and keep it there for 20 minutes. Carefully release the steam and pressure when opening the lid. The meat should be soft and tender. Set the meat and stock aside.

Add the oil to a medium pot over high heat and fry the onions, stirring occasionally, for 5 minutes, or until golden brown. Stir in the tomatoes, mung beans, and 6 cups (1.5 liters) water, bring to a boil, and cook for 10–12 minutes, or until the mung beans are parboiled (softened slightly, but not mushy).

Add the rice to the pot, along with the meat and all its stock, the chili, cumin, coriander, dill, boiling water, and 2 teaspoons salt. Bring back to a boil and cook for 5 minutes, then reduce the heat to medium and stir to combine. Cover with a lid and cook for 20 minutes.

Reduce the heat to very low and simmer for 10 minutes, or until the rice has absorbed all the liquid. At this stage, do not mix the rice anymore, or it will break and change the texture of the dish. It should be sticky and soft, but not mushy, and the meat should be soft and tender. Serve immediately on a large platter.

KOFTA CHALLAW

کوفته چلو

4 large ripe tomatoes, quartered
1 garlic clove, coarsely chopped
½ cup (125 ml) sunflower oil
1 large yellow onion, finely diced
1 teaspoon white sugar
1 teaspoon curry powder
2½ tablespoons white vinegar
Heaped 1 tablespoon tomato paste
Challaw (see page 111), to serve

FOR THE KOFTA
1 large yellow onion, coarsely chopped
1 long fresh red chili, coarsely chopped
Fresh cilantro, leaves and stems coarsely
  chopped, plus extra leaves to serve
1 garlic clove, coarsely chopped
9 oz (250 g) fatty ground lamb
9 oz (250 g) lean ground beef
1 teaspoon coriander seeds, ground in
  a spice grinder or mortar and pestle
Salt and freshly ground black pepper

The kofta, or meatballs, in this dish are made using a combination of lamb and beef. They're not the round balls usually associated with kofta, but a slightly flat patty shape, which is common in Afghan cuisine. They are cooked in a tomato and onion sauce and traditionally served with challaw rice.

To make the kofta, finely blend the onion, chili, cilantro, and garlic in a food processor. Add ¼ cup (60 ml) water and blend again to form a fine paste. Place the lamb and beef in a large bowl, add the blended paste, the ground coriander, 2 teaspoons salt, and 1 teaspoon freshly ground black pepper. Using your hands, mix to combine for 5 minutes, or until the ingredients are fully incorporated and the mixture is slightly sticky. Divide the meat mixture into 12 equal portions and shape into 3 in (7.5 cm) patties. Place the patties on a tray lined with parchment paper and refrigerate for at least 30 minutes to become slightly firm.

Meanwhile, finely blend the tomatoes and garlic in a food processor. Heat the oil in a large saucepan over high heat and fry the onion, stirring occasionally, for 5 minutes, or until golden brown. Add the blended tomatoes and garlic, and fry with the onion for 2 minutes, or until fragrant. Stir in the sugar, curry powder, vinegar, and 2 teaspoons salt, or to taste, and cook for another minute. Add the tomato paste and mix well to combine. Finally, add 3 cups (750 ml) water, bring the sauce to a boil, then reduce the heat to medium.

Add the kofta to the sauce, shaking the pan gently from side to side to make sure they are submerged. Increase the heat to high, bring to a boil, then reduce the heat to medium. Cover with a lid and simmer for 20–25 minutes, or until the sauce has reduced and thickened, and is rich in color. Serve the kofta over freshly cooked challaw and garnished with cilantro leaves.

MAASH PALAW

This palaw, studded with mung beans and raisins, was one our favorites as children. The mung beans give the maash palaw a subtle earthy flavor and, with the sweetness of the raisins, it is a balanced dish that's hard to resist.

You need to soak the rice for at least 2–3 hours before preparing this palaw.

1 cup (8 oz/225 g) mung beans
2 cups (14 oz/400 g) sella basmati rice, soaked for 2-3 hours
¾ cup (185 ml) sunflower oil
2 medium yellow onions, finely diced
Heaped 1 cup (6 oz/170 g) raisins or golden raisins
2 teaspoons ground cumin
Salt

Bring 8½ cups (2 liters) water to a boil in a large pot. Add the mung beans and boil for 20 minutes, or until parboiled.

Drain the rice and add it to the pot with the mung beans. Add 1 tablespoon salt and bring to a boil, then cook for 8–10 minutes, or until parboiled and the grains seem to have doubled in length. Drain the rice and beans in a colander, then return to the pot.

Add the oil to a small saucepan over high heat and fry the onions for 5 minutes, or until golden brown. Tip the onions and oil into the pot with the rice, and add the raisins. Add 1 tablespoon salt and 1 cup (250 ml) boiling water and, using a kafgeer or large flat slotted spoon, mix gently to combine. Sprinkle the cumin over the rice and cover with a lid. Cook over high heat for 6–8 minutes, or until steam escapes from under the lid, then reduce the heat to low and cook for 20 minutes.

Transfer the maash palaw to a large platter, creating a heap studded with mung beans and raisins, then serve immediately.

RESHTAH PALAW

9 oz (250 g) vermicelli noodles made
  with eggs
3 cups (1 lb 5 oz/600 g) sella basmati
  rice, soaked for 2-3 hours
¾ cup (185 ml) sunflower oil
1 large yellow onion, finely diced
Salt

This rice dish includes thin noodles. Traditionally in Afghanistan they would have been made from scratch. Over time, however, it has become common and convenient to use store-bought vermicelli pasta, which is dry-roasted before being cooked with the rice. Soak the rice for at least 2-3 hours beforehand.

Gently break the noodles into short lengths in a large bowl; if the vermicelli is coiled, break it up so that the lengths are straight. Place a large frying pan over high heat for 2-3 minutes, until the base is hot, then reduce the heat to medium. Add the noodles and gently dry-roast them in small batches for 5 minutes per batch, or until golden brown. Remove them from the pan and set aside.

Bring 12 cups (3 liters) water to a boil in a large pot. Drain the rice and rinse under cold running water until the water runs clear. Add 2½ tablespoons salt and the rice to the boiling water and cook for 6-8 minutes, or until parboiled and the grains seem to have doubled in length. Add the noodles to the pot and boil for a further 2 minutes. Now drain the rice and noodles in a colander, discarding the water, and return to the pot.

In a small saucepan, heat the oil over high heat for 2 minutes. Add the onion and fry for 3-4 minutes, or until golden brown. Add 1½ cups (375 ml) water and bring to a boil, then remove from the heat. Add this to the rice and noodle mixture and use a kafgeer or large flat slotted spoon to mix gently, taking care not to break the noodles or the rice. Cover with a lid and cook over high heat for 5-6 minutes, or until steam starts to escape from under the lid; it's important to keep an eye out for the steam to avoid overcooking the rice. Reduce the heat to low and cook for a further 15 minutes.

Serve on a large platter, alongside your favorite qormah curry (see pages 176, 183, and 184).

MORGH PALAW

Morgh palaw, a delicious rice dish with chicken buried beneath, is prepared using a richly flavored chicken stock called yakhni morgh. It is beautifully decorated with cranberries and saffron-infused rice. Soak the rice for at least 2–3 hours beforehand.

◆

To make the yakhni morgh, preheat the oven to 425°F (220°C). Place the onion in a roasting pan and rest the chicken on top. Rub the oil and 1 tablespoon salt over the chicken and roast for 30–40 minutes, or until it is golden brown and the onion is caramelized. Transfer to a pressure cooker and pour in 10 cups (2.5 liters) water. Seal with the lid and bring it to high pressure over high heat. Once the pressure cooker is whistling, reduce the heat to low and cook slowly for 30 minutes. Carefully remove the lid. Discard the chicken carcass and strain the stock into a bowl—you should have about 4¼ cups (1 liter).

For the palaw, gently rub 1 teaspoon salt all over the chicken. Add the oil to a medium pot over high heat and fry the chicken on all sides, until the meat is seared and slightly browned. With the chicken breast-side up, add 3½ cups (875 ml) yakhni morgh (refrigerate remaining stock for 3 days or freeze for a month) to the pot, bring to a boil, and reduce the heat to low. Cook for 15 minutes, then flip the chicken over and cook for another 15 minutes, or until cooked through. Remove the chicken, cover, and set aside. Keep the stock in the pot to pour over the rice.

Drain any excess water from the rice and rinse under cold running water until the water runs clear. Bring 10 cups (2.5 liters) water to a boil in

FOR THE YAKHNI MORGH (CHICKEN STOCK)
1 large yellow onion, finely diced
2¼ lb (1 kg) whole chicken, skin removed
2½ tablespoons sunflower oil

FOR THE PALAW
2¼ lb (1 kg) whole chicken, skin removed
½ cup (125 ml) sunflower oil, plus
  1 tablespoon extra
3 cups (1 lb 5 oz/600 g) sella basmati
  rice, soaked for 2-3 hours
1 teaspoon ground cardamom
1 teaspoon cumin seeds

FOR THE TOPPING
½ teaspoon saffron threads
1 tablespoon sunflower oil
½ cup (1¾ oz/50 g) dried cranberries
1 teaspoon white sugar

a large pot. Add 1 teaspoon salt and the rice, and boil for 6-8 minutes, or until the rice is parboiled and the grains have doubled in length. Drain the rice in a colander and return to the pot. Pour the reserved stock over the rice and mix gently—there should be about ½ in (1 cm) of stock in the bottom of the pot with the rice. Add the extra oil and gently mix. Create a well in the center of the rice and place the chicken in the well. Cover with rice and sprinkle with the cardamom and cumin. Cover the pot with a lid and cook over high heat until steam escapes from under the lid, then reduce the heat to low and cook for 20 minutes.

Make the topping about 10 minutes before serving. Place the saffron in a small bowl with 1 tablespoon boiling water for 5 minutes, or until it releases its color. Put the oil and cranberries into a small saucepan and stir over medium heat for 1 minute, no longer, just to heat through. Remove the pan from the heat and sprinkle in the sugar, then stir in a large spoonful of cooked rice. Add the saffron water, and stir to color the rice.

To serve, spoon some rice onto a large platter, then break or cut the chicken into pieces and place on top. Finish with the saffron rice and cranberry topping.

◆ ◆

SHALGHAM CHALLAW

This turnip and lamb curry is served atop a bed of challaw and is traditionally made in winter when turnips are in season in Afghanistan. It is hearty comfort food.

This dish is prepared using a pressure cooker to soften the lamb to a tender consistency.

1 cup (250 ml) sunflower oil
3 large yellow onions, diced
2¼ lb (1 kg) lamb shoulder pieces, bone in
2 lb 4 oz (1 kg) turnips, each peeled
  and diced into 8 pieces
Heaped 1 tablespoon ground red pepper
Heaped 1 tablespoon finely grated
  fresh ginger
2 teaspoons light brown sugar
Challaw (see page 111), to serve
Salt

Heat the oil in the pan of a pressure cooker over high heat, add the onions, and fry for 5 minutes, or until golden brown. Add the lamb and fry, stirring occasionally, for 5 minutes, or until the meat is seared and browned all over. Add 1 tablespoon salt and 2 cups (500 ml) water, and place the lid on the pressure cooker, sealing it shut. Bring the cooker to high pressure and keep it there for 25 minutes. Carefully release the steam from the cooker before removing the lid. The lamb should be tender on the bone.

Add the turnips, ground red pepper, ginger, sugar, and 1½ cups (375 ml) water to the lamb and cook over medium heat in the pressure cooker, uncovered, for a further 10–12 minutes, or until the lamb and turnips are cooked through and tender, but not falling apart.

Serve shalgham with steaming hot challaw.

SHAAMI KEBAB

شامی کباب

1 lb 2 oz (500 g) diced boneless lamb leg
1 lb 2 oz (500 g) diced boneless beef rump
3 medium all-purpose potatoes, peeled
   and quartered
3 small yellow onions, peeled and
   quartered
5 garlic cloves, coarsely chopped
1 moderately hot fresh red chili, chopped
Small handful fresh cilantro, leaves and
   stalks finely chopped
2 teaspoons ground turmeric
2 teaspoons ground ginger
1 teaspoon ground coriander
1 teaspoon ground cumin
1 egg
Sunflower oil, for deep-frying
Salt and freshly ground black pepper

Traditionally a dish for festive occasions, such as birthday and engagement parties, shaami kebab is a type of fried Afghan kebab served with hand-cut potato fries, dusted in salt, or vinegar and spices. After creating a paste from meat, vegetables, herbs, and spices, shaami kebabs are then fried, giving them their unique texture—a delicate crisp shell and melt-in-the-mouth insides.

◆

Combine the lamb, beef, potatoes, onions, and garlic in a medium pot with 5¼ cups (1.25 liters) water, bring to a boil, and cover with a lid. Boil until the potatoes are cooked through and easy to mash, 10–12 minutes. Using tongs or a slotted spoon, transfer the potatoes to a bowl, mash until smooth, and set aside to cool. Boil the remaining ingredients in the saucepan, uncovered, until the liquid has totally evaporated, then leave to cool completely. Once cooled, blend to a smooth paste in a food processor and transfer to a bowl.

Add the chili, cilantro, mashed potatoes, spices, 1 teaspoon black pepper, and 2 teaspoons salt to the paste. Using your hands, mix for 5 minutes, or until all the ingredients are thoroughly combined. Crack the egg into the bowl and continue mixing by hand for another 5 minutes, or until the mixture is well combined and sticky.

Divide the meat mixture into roughly 20 equal portions. Lightly grease your hands to prevent sticking, then take one portion and squeeze it between your hands several times to ensure it keeps its form when fried. Gradually form a tapered oblong shape, about 4 in (10 cm) long and set aside on a tray lined with parchment paper. Repeat with the remaining portions.

In a medium saucepan, heat enough oil for deep-frying over high heat to 350°F (180°C) on an oil thermometer.

Fry the kebabs in batches of 3 or 4 at a time, for 2–3 minutes each side, or until crisp and golden to dark brown. Gently remove the shaami kebabs with a slotted spoon and set aside on a plate lined with paper towels to drain. Serve immediately to savor the crunch, but these can also be enjoyed cold.

ROHT

⅔ cup (170 ml) lukewarm milk
2 large eggs
½ cup (125 ml) sunflower oil
2½ cups (10½ oz/300 g) self-rising flour,
  plus more for dusting
2½ cups (10½ oz/300 g) whole-wheat flour
1¾ cups (11½ oz/330 g) superfine sugar
2 teaspoons ground cardamom
1 teaspoon baking soda
2½ tablespoons milk powder
1 teaspoon white poppyseeds
1 teaspoon black poppyseeds
Salt

In Afghanistan, this popular sweet bread is made for birthday and engagement parties. People would make the roht dough at home and send it with one of the children in the family to the local bakery, where the daash waan, or baker, would roll and intricately decorate the roht before baking it perfectly in a special oven. It would be picked up a couple of hours later and taken home to cut and enjoy as part of the celebratory spread.

Whisk together the milk, eggs, and oil in a bowl. Place the remaining ingredients, except the poppyseeds, in a separate bowl with ¼ teaspoon salt and whisk to combine.

In the center of the dry ingredients, create a well with your hand and gradually add the wet ingredients to the well, mixing by hand to combine until a soft, sticky dough forms.

Lightly dust your work surface with flour and turn out the dough onto it. Lightly and quickly knead the dough for 2 minutes, or until soft and elastic. Place it in a clean bowl, cover with a tea towel, and set aside for 10 minutes to rest. Meanwhile, preheat the oven to 350°F (180°C) and line two baking pans with parchment paper.

Once the dough is rested, divide it in two and use your hands to spread and flatten each portion on each tray into a rough circle about 8 in (20 cm) in diameter with an even thickness. Sprinkle the poppyseeds on top, then place the pans in the oven and bake the roht for 25–30 minutes, or until golden brown.

Transfer to a wire rack to cool completely before cutting into wedges to serve. Roht will keep for 2–3 days stored in an airtight container.

From left to right:
Shaami kebab (page 131);
Qaymaq chai (page 136);
Roht (page 132)

QAYMAQ CHAI

قیماق چای

1 cup (3 oz/85 g) loose-leaf green tea
10 cups (2.5 liters) hot water
2 teaspoons baking soda
⅔ cup (160 ml) chilled water
6 cups (1.5 liters) whole milk
1¾ cups (11½ oz/330 g) sugar
2 teaspoons ground cardamom
Qaymaq or clotted cream, to serve

Qaymaq chai is a beautifully soft-pink toned milk tea, with qaymaq, or clotted cream, on top. It is rich and sweet, and reserved for special occasions because making it involves quite an elaborate process called baad kaash. This method is used to aerate the tea and deepen its red color, which softens to a light-pink shade with the addition of milk.

The qaymaq cream also takes some time to prepare: it is made by bringing milk to a boil in a large shallow pan, then simmering it for hours while repeatedly skimming off (and keeping) the layers of cream that rise to the surface, until there is no more to collect. In Afghanistan, people normally buy qaymaq from deli-type grocers; elsewhere, it can sometimes be found in Persian and Middle Eastern grocery shops. The cream can be added or left out, depending on taste.

Too rich and heavy to drink in the morning or late in the evening, qaymaq chai is traditionally only consumed in the afternoon with some roht or other light snacks, such as kolcheh Nowrozi (see page 29) or dried fruit and nuts.

To make qaymaq chai, you will need a cup of chilled water ready in the fridge, or just add some ice to a cup of cold water.

Bring the tea and hot water to a boil in a saucepan, then reduce the heat to low and simmer for 20 minutes. Add the baking soda and simmer for a further 5 minutes, or until the tea has turned an orange-reddish color. Put 2½ tablespoons chilled water into a stainless-steel bowl. Strain the boiled tea through a colander into the bowl and discard the leaves.

Put 2½ tablespoons chilled water into another similar-sized bowl and, holding the bowl with the tea at arm's length above, pour it steadily into the bowl with the chilled water to combine and then back again; this is called baad kaash. Repeat this process twice, each time adding 2½ tablespoons chilled water to the empty bowl. Continue transferring the tea between the bowls another 11 times, without adding any more chilled water, until the tea resembles the deep red color of pomegranate juice.

To make the chai, add 2 cups (500 ml) of the red tea to a large saucepan with the milk, sugar, and cardamom over high heat, stirring to dissolve the sugar. Bring to a boil, then reduce the heat to low and simmer for 5 minutes, or until the mixture develops a soft pink tone. Ladle the qaymaq chai into cups and, if desired, add a dollop of qaymaq or clotted cream to each cup. Serve hot.

This recipe makes 6 cups (1.5 liters) red tea; the remainder can be refrigerated for 1–2 weeks in a sealed jar or frozen for up to 3 months, ready to make more batches of qaymaq chai.

MAGHOOT

ماغوت

½ cup (2 oz/60 g) cornstarch
½ cup (3½ oz/100 g) sugar
¼ cup (60 ml) rosewater
2 teaspoons food coloring of choice
4¼ cups (1 liter) hot water
¼ cup (1 oz/30 g) slivered pistachios
Small handful of dried rose petals

Maghoot is a type of jello-like sweet dish traditionally made for celebratory events such as weddings. The ingredients are simple, and it can be made in an array of colors, making it a sweet, simple, and festive addition to the dessert table.

Whisk the cornstarch and sugar in a mixing bowl to combine. Add the rosewater, your choice of food coloring, and ½ cup (125 ml) water. Whisk to form a smooth slurry and set aside.

Bring the hot water to a boil in a medium pot, then remove it from the heat. Add a ladleful to the cornstarch slurry, and whisk until smooth and combined. Adding the boiling water to the slurry in this way helps to temper it and prevent lumps in the custard.

Slowly add the tempered slurry to the remaining boiling water, whisking continuously, until all of it has been added and combined. Place the pot over medium heat and stir continuously until the maghoot begins to bubble.

Working quickly, pour it into a serving dish (or dishes) and sprinkle with slivered pistachios and dried rose petals. Carefully place in the fridge and chill for at least 3 hours before serving.

From left to right:
Maghoot (page 137);
Firni (page 141);
Rose sharbat (page 140)

ROSE SHARBAT

Made during the hot summer months and also during Ramadan, the Muslim month of fasting, rose sharbat is a sweet rose-infused drink. It's fragrantly floral and refreshing, and also infused with basil seeds, which add a jelly-like texture to the drink.

```
2⅓ cups (15½ oz/440 g) white sugar
¼ cup (60 ml) rosewater
2 teaspoons red or pink food coloring
Heaped 1 tablespoon dried basil
  seeds (sabja), available from
  Asian grocery shops
2 cups (500 ml) boiling water
Chilled water, to serve
```

Stir the sugar, rosewater, food coloring, and 1½ cups (375 ml) water in a saucepan over high heat to dissolve the sugar. Bring to a boil, then reduce the heat to medium and simmer for 5 minutes, or until a slightly thickened syrup forms and the temperature reads 233°F (112°C) on a candy thermometer. Set aside to cool.

Pour the boiling water into a bowl and stir in the basil seeds, then set aside for at least 10 minutes to cool. The seeds will soak up the water, becoming sticky and gelatinous.

To serve, put 2½ tablespoons of the cooled syrup into a tall glass. Add ice, fill with chilled water, and stir in a teaspoon of soaked basil seeds.

The syrup and soaked basil seeds will keep in the fridge for a week, ready to make more sharbat.

FIRNI

فرنی

2½ tablespoons cornstarch
½ cup (3½ oz/100 g) sugar
1 teaspoon ground cardamom
4¼ cups (1 liter) whole milk
¼ cup (1 oz/30 g) slivered pistachios
Small handful dried rose petals

Firni is a traditional Afghan milk custard, smooth and delicately spiced with cardamom. Although it can be made for all kinds of gatherings, it's always prepared as part of the bridal table dessert spread. Once the custard is set, it can be layered with all kinds of toppings, including maghoot (see page 137), fruit compotes, and nuts; this recipe uses slivered pistachios and rose petals.

Add the cornstarch, sugar, and cardamom to a bowl and whisk to combine. Add ¼ cup (60 ml) water, whisk well to form a smooth slurry, and set aside.

Bring the milk to just below boiling in a medium saucepan over high heat. Watch for the milk bubbling and, just before it does, remove the pan from the heat. Add a ladleful of the hot milk to the cornstarch slurry and whisk until smooth. Adding the hot milk to the slurry in this way helps to temper it and prevent lumps in the custard.

Slowly add the tempered slurry to the remaining hot milk, whisking continuously until all of it has been added and combined. Place the saucepan over medium heat and stir continuously until the firni begins to bubble. Working quickly, pour it into serving bowls and sprinkle with slivered pistachios and dried rose petals. Carefully place the firni in the fridge for at least 3 hours to chill completely before serving.

GOSHEH FIL

گوش فیل

Gosheh fil is a crumbly pastry dessert, dusted with cardamom and ground pistachios. The name translates directly to "elephant ears" because of its shape. These pastries are a favorite during the Muslim festival of Eid.

3 large eggs
¼ cup (60 ml) sunflower oil
3 cups (13 oz/375 g) all-purpose flour, plus extra for dusting
½ teaspoon baking powder
¼ cup (60 ml) warm whole milk
Sunflower oil for deep-frying
2 cups (9 oz/250 g) confectioners' sugar
4 teaspoons ground cardamom
¼ cup (1 oz/30 g) ground pistachios
Salt

Crack the eggs into a bowl and, while whisking continuously, slowly add the oil until combined.

In a separate bowl, whisk the flour, baking powder, and ½ teaspoon salt to combine. Make a well in the center and pour in the egg mixture. Mix to combine with your hands, then add the milk and continue mixing to just bring together.

Lightly dust a work surface with flour, turn out the dough, and knead for 6–8 minutes, or until smooth and firm. Divide the dough into two equal balls, cover, and leave to rest for 30 minutes.

Lightly dust the cleaned work surface and roll out each dough ball to a paper-thin, almost translucent sheet of pastry. Using a large cookie cutter 3½–4 in (8–10 cm) in diameter, cut out circles, then pinch each circle at one point to form a fanned ear shape.

In a saucepan, heat enough oil for deep-frying to 315°F (160°C) on an oil thermometer.

Fry the pastries in batches, turning occasionally, until light golden and bubbles have formed on both sides. Using a slotted spoon, transfer the pastries to a tray lined with paper towels to absorb the excess oil.

Arrange the gosheh fil on a serving platter, and sprinkle generously with the confectioners' sugar, cardamom, and ground pistachios.

KHAJOOR

3 cups (13 oz/370 g) all-purpose flour
½ cup (2½ oz/70 g) self-rising whole-wheat
  flour (or self-rising white flour if
  you can't find whole-wheat)
Generous 1 cup (8 oz/225 g) superfine
  sugar
1 teaspoon ground cardamom, plus extra
  to serve
4 tablespoons (1½ oz/40 g) butter
2½ tablespoons canola oil, plus extra
  for deep-frying
3 eggs
¼ cup (60 ml) whole milk

These are a type of fried cookie flavored with cardamom. Made using basic ingredients and equipment, khajoor is simple and rustic fare, traditionally made in the countryside of Afghanistan. My mother remembers eating them when visiting family or friends in the rural province of Laghman.

◆

Whisk the flours, sugar, and cardamom in a bowl to combine. Add the butter and oil, and rub in with your hands until the mixture resembles breadcrumbs.

In a separate bowl, whisk the eggs and milk until frothy. Add the egg mixture to the flour mixture, mix with your hands to combine, and knead to form a sticky ball of dough. Cover with a tea towel and set aside at room temperature for 10 minutes to rest.

Once rested, the dough should be smooth and firm; if it's still sticky, add a light dusting of flour and knead to combine. Break off a golf ball-sized piece of dough. This next part is what gives the khajoor its shape, and it can be a bit tricky to perfect; it requires a technique similar to rolling gnocchi. Roll the piece of dough on the inside of a colander to form an oblong shape imprinted with the grid-like pattern from the colander. Set aside on a tray lined with parchment paper and repeat with the remaining dough.

In a heavy-based saucepan or wok, heat enough oil for deep-frying to 315–325°F (160–170°C) on an oil thermometer.

Fry 5 or 6 khajoors at a time, turning occasionally with a slotted spoon, for 5–6 minutes, or until they are golden brown all over. Make sure to test the inside is cooked through and not doughy.

Transfer the fried khajoors to a plate lined with paper towels to drain the excess oil and set aside at room temperature to cool. Sprinkle with ground cardamom and serve. Khajoors keep well in a sealed container for a week.

KHETAYEE

خَتایئ

2½ cups (10½ oz/300 g) all-purpose flour
Scant 1 cup (4 oz/113 g) whole
  milk powder
1 teaspoon baking powder
1 cup (4½ oz/125 g) confectioners' sugar
1⅓ cups (310 ml) warm canola oil
¼ cup (1 oz/30 g) ground pistachios

These traditional cookies are usually made during Eid celebrations in Afghanistan. During my parents' time there, people bought these from the local bakeries called kulchah feroshees, which used age-old techniques, and had special ovens to bake cookies and pastries to perfection.

Preheat the oven to 300°F (150°C).

Add all the ingredients, except the oil and pistachios, to a bowl and mix to combine well. Slowly add the oil and, using your hands, mix to form a soft but firm dough.

Divide the dough into 12 equal portions and roll them into smooth balls between your palms. Arrange them, well spaced apart, on a baking pan lined with parchment paper and press each ball with your hand to flatten slightly. Make an indent in the center of each cookie with your thumb, then bake on the middle shelf in the oven for 20 minutes, or until they are light golden.

Cool the khetayee briefly on the pan before transferring them to a wire rack. Sprinkle a small pinch of ground pistachios into the indent of each cookie to decorate, and serve when they are completely cooled. Khetayee can be stored for 3–4 days in an airtight container.

CREAM ROLLS

کریسم رول

2 cups (9 oz/250 g) all-purpose flour
1 cup (9 oz/250 g) butter, at room
  temperature, cut into small cubes
⅔ cup (150 ml) chilled water
Scant ½ cup (1¾ oz/50 g) ground pistachios
Small handful of dried rose petals
Salt

FOR THE FILLING
3¾ cups (900 ml) heavy whipping cream
¼ cup (1 oz/30 g) confectioners' sugar,
  plus 2 cups (9 oz/250 g) extra for rolling
1 teaspoon ground cardamom

When my parents were living in Afghanistan, these light, crisp, cream-filled pastry horns were bought from special patisseries known as kulchah feroshees. They are usually served during celebrations such as Eid or for birthdays.

This recipe is my sister Fatema's; guided by my mother, the flavors of Afghanistan, and her natural talent, she has become an expert sweet maker.

◆

Whisk the flour and 1 teaspoon salt in a bowl to combine. Add the butter and, using your fingertips, quickly and loosely rub the butter into the flour. You still want to see bits of the butter in the flour, so take care not to overwork.

Create a well in the center of the flour and pour in the chilled water. Using your hands, mix the ingredients to combine and form a firm but rough dough. Cover the dough with a tea towel and refrigerate for 25–30 minutes to chill. Dust a work surface with flour, turn out the chilled dough, and knead gently until smooth. Work the dough into a rectangular shape by hand, then roll with a rolling pin in one direction to make a rectangle roughly 20 in x 8 in (50 cm x 20 cm). Streaks of butter should be visible, indicating that it hasn't been overworked. Fold the top third down to the center and fold the bottom third up to overlap. Turn the dough 90 degrees, either to the left or right, and roll again to a 20 in x 8 in (50 cm x 20 cm) rectangle. Repeat this folding and rolling one more time, then cover with a tea towel and refrigerate for 25–30 minutes to chill.

Meanwhile, preheat the oven to 350°F (180°C). Divide the chilled dough into 3 equal portions. Lightly dust your work surface with flour and roll 1 portion to a rectangle about 10 in x 8 in (25 cm x 20 cm) and about ⅛ in (3 mm) thick. Cut 1 in (2.5 cm) wide strips along the length of the rectangle so that each strip is 10 in (25 cm) long.

Lightly grease some cannoli tubes with oil and wrap a strip of pastry around the length of one tube in a spiral, overlapping as you go, to ensure there are no gaps. Repeat the same process with the remaining 2 portions of dough.

Place the tubes on a baking pan lined with parchment paper and bake for 20–25 minutes, or until golden brown. Place each cannoli tube with the pastry wrapped around it on a wire rack to cool for an hour or so, before gently separating the pastries from the tubes.

While the pastries are cooling, prepare the cream filling. Add the cream, confectioners' sugar, and cardamom to the bowl of an electric mixer fitted with a balloon whisk, and whip until stiff peaks form. Place the cream into a pastry bag and pipe it into the cooled pastries to fill. Place the extra confectioners' sugar in a bowl and roll the filled pastries in the sugar, to coat all sides. Serve, sprinkled with the pistachios and dried rose petals.

Cream rolls are best enjoyed fresh, on the day they are made.

From top left:
Kulcheh shor (page 155);
Kulcheh chaarmaghzi (page 157);
Khetayee (page 146);
Khajoor (page 145)

From bottom right:
Cream rolls (page 149);
Gosheh fil (page 142)

SHIRPERA

شیر پیره

2⅓ cups (15½ oz/440 g) sugar
2 teaspoons ground cardamom
1 tablespoon rosewater
1 tablespoon butter
1 cup (3½ oz/100 g) slivered almonds
Scant ½ cup (1¾ oz/50 g) coarsely chopped
  pistachios
5½ cups (1 lb 7½ oz/670 g) whole
  milk powder
Scant ½ cup (1¾ oz/50 g) finely chopped
  pistachios
Handful of slivered pistachios,
  to decorate

Shirpera is a nut-filled sweet with a texture that sits somewhere between a crumbly nougat and fudge. In Afghanistan, during celebrations such as Eid, people usually buy shirpera from specialty sweet shops called qanadis, which sell different types of sweets such as halwa, hard candies, chocolates, and sugared almonds called noql. Shirpera requires overnight resting for the sweet to fully set. This is one of my sister Fatema's recipes.

Lightly grease a 12 in x 8 in (30 cm x 20 cm) sheet cake pan and line it with parchment paper overhanging at each end to help lift out the shirpera when it has set.

Mix the sugar and 1 cup (250 ml) water in a saucepan over high heat to dissolve the sugar. Bring to a boil and cook without stirring for 5 minutes, or until the syrup thickens and reaches between 225–233°F (110–112°C) on a candy thermometer.

Remove the pan from the heat and pour the syrup into a large bowl. Add the cardamom, rosewater, butter, almonds, and coarsely chopped pistachios. Mix to combine using a wooden spoon, then add the milk powder in batches, mixing to incorporate between additions. It's important to work quickly when stirring in the milk powder because, as the mixture cools between each addition, it will become firmer and more difficult to mix. The consistency of the finished mixture should be thick and soft, but holding its form, rather than runny or very hard when poured from a spoon.

Spread the mixture evenly in the pan using a metal spatula, then dampen your hands and smooth the surface. Sprinkle the finely chopped pistachios over the top, gently pushing them into the fudge. Decorate with slivered pistachios, then set aside overnight, uncovered, at room temperature to completely set and become firm.

Traditionally, shirpera is cut into diamond shapes or squares and piled high on decorative platters to serve. It can be refrigerated in an airtight container for up to 2 weeks.

KULCHEH SHOR

Kulcheh shor are savory cookies, traditionally made during Eid. They are slightly salty with a crumbly texture somewhere between bread and a cookie. Kulcheh shor are quite thick, with a nest-like appearance, and nigella seeds sprinkled on top to decorate.

3 cups (13 oz/370 g) all-purpose flour
⅓ cup (2¾ oz/80 g) low-sodium margarine, at room temperature
2 large eggs, lightly beaten
⅔ cup (160 ml) lukewarm water
Milk, for brushing
2½ tablespoons nigella seeds
Salt

Preheat the oven to 350°F (180°C) and line a baking pan with parchment paper.

Whisk the flour, and 1 teaspoon salt in a bowl to combine. Add the margarine and rub in with your fingertips until the mixture resembles fine breadcrumbs.

Make a well in the center of the mixture, and add the egg and water to the well. Mix to combine with your hands to form a firm dough. Knead for 3–4 minutes, or until the dough is firm, elastic, and not sticky. Cover with a tea towel and set aside to rest for 10 minutes. Once rested, divide the dough into 12 equal portions and shape into smooth balls by rolling between your palms.

To form the special nest shape, hold a ball of dough gently between your fingers and thumb, then run the tip of a small knife gently around edge, as you spin the ball. Gently indent the center with your thumb, flattening the ball slightly and creating a well in the center. Place the cookies on the baking pan as you form them, brush the tops with milk, and sprinkle nigella seeds into the centers.

Bake the cookies on the middle shelf in the oven for 30 minutes, or until kulcheh shor are light golden. Cool them briefly on the pan, then transfer them to a wire rack to cool completely before serving. Kulcheh shor can be stored for 1 week in an airtight container.

KULCHEH BADAMI

کلچه بادامی

Another Eid celebration favorite is kulcheh badami—sweet, nutty cookies with a crumbly texture that are usually served alongside piles of other traditional sweets to mark the celebratory feast.

1 cup (9 oz/250 g) butter, at room temperature
2 cups (9 oz/250 g) confectioners' sugar
2 large eggs, at room temperature
2½ cups (10½ oz/300 g) self-rising flour
2½ cups (10½ oz/300 g) all-purpose flour
1½ cups (5¼ oz/150 g) coarsely chopped almonds

Preheat the oven to 350°F (180°C) and line a baking pan with parchment paper.

Cream the butter and sugar in the bowl of an electric mixer fitted with the paddle attachment until pale and creamy. Add the eggs one at a time, beating between each addition to incorporate well.

Stop the mixer and, using your hands, gently fold in first the flours and then the almonds to form a soft, sticky dough.

Divide the dough into 12 equal portions with a spoon then, with slightly damp hands to prevent sticking, shape them into smooth round balls, placing them on the baking pan as you go. Gently press each one with your hand to flatten slightly, and bake on the middle shelf in the oven for 20 minutes, or until they are light golden.

Cool briefly on the pan, then transfer the cookies to a wire rack to cool completely before serving. Kulcheh badami can be stored for 1 week in an airtight container.

KULCHEH CHAARMAGHZI

کلچہ چار مغزی

With a hint of cinnamon, kulcheh chaarmaghzi are beautifully fragrant and sweet crumbly cookies made with walnuts. They usually adorn the Eid celebration spread.

½ cup (4 oz/113 g) butter, at room temperature
1 cup (4½ oz/125 g) confectioners' sugar
1 large egg, at room temperature
1 cup (5¼ oz/150 g) self-rising flour
1¼ cups (5¼ oz/150 g) all-purpose flour
2 teaspoons ground cinnamon
1 cup (4 oz/120 g) finely chopped walnuts
1 tablespoon whole milk
Salt

Preheat the oven to 350°F (180°C) and line a baking pan with parchment paper.

Cream the butter and sugar in the bowl of an electric mixer fitted with the paddle attachment until pale and creamy. Add the egg, beating to incorporate well.

Stop the mixer and, using your hands, gently fold in the flours, cinnamon, and a pinch of salt, followed by the walnuts. Add the milk and knead gently to form a soft, sticky dough.

Divide the dough into 12 equal portions with a spoon then, with slightly damp hands to prevent sticking, shape them into smooth round balls, placing them on the baking pan as you go. Gently press each one with your hand to flatten slightly, then bake on the middle shelf in the oven for 20 minutes, or until they are a light golden.

Cool briefly on the pan, then transfer the cookies to a wire rack to cool completely before serving. Kulcheh chaarmaghzi can be stored for 1 week in an airtight container.

Chapter 4

The Plight of the Displaced

فصل چهارم

RECONCILING BINARIES

فَرْهاد صَميع

"Your joy is your sorrow unmasked.
And the selfsame well from which your laughter rises was oftentimes filled with your tears.
And how else can it be?
The deeper that sorrow carves into your being, the more joy you can contain.
Is not the cup that holds your wine the very cup that was burned in the potter's oven?
And is not the lute that soothes your spirit, the very wood that was hollowed with knives?
When you are joyous, look deep into your heart and you shall find it is only that which has given you sorrow that is giving you joy.
When you are sorrowful look again in your heart, and you shall see that in truth you are weeping for that which has been your delight."

Kahlil Gibran, *The Prophet*, 1923

The physical displacement of my family from Afghanistan was made possible by the long era of spiritual and psychological displacement that preceded it. The aura of the nation had been scrambled, caught between the ideological binaries imposed upon it. Communists and increasingly fundamentalist Islamists fought to control it, using the same instruments of blunt force. Against the backdrop of the Cold War, more and more foreign interests intervened and attempted to manipulate the conflict in Afghanistan in ways that would best meet their own needs. In a world becoming more interconnected and globalized, with increasing stores of power liberated through energy and technological, militaristic, and scientific revolutions, the consequences of conflict for Afghanistan and its people became increasingly dire.

In the ongoing conflict, and with a huge portion of its population exiled, by the 1980s Afghanistan had been stripped bare of its cultural and spiritual essence. By the time my family arrived in Australia, living as displaced people, we had a collection of wounds to heal. Finding sanctuary gave us the means necessary to dream again, but these dreams were deeply attached to the mourning of all that had been lost. The call upon us was to find the means to reconcile our seemingly disparate worlds. Time and again, a natural conduit for this negotiation was food. On lands far from our ancestral home, the profundity of remembering through food would bind us. Years later, when Parwana first opened its doors, it was through a process of internal reconciliation

that we would create something as an offering to those in our new home. Parwana was an outward expression of the impression on our souls of the combined weight of our history, our family story, and our aspirations for, and pledges to, tomorrow.

Becoming refugees

Our stepping from Afghanistan across the border into Pakistan at the Khyber Pass in 1985 was significant on several levels. Firstly, it was the moment we became refugees. The long and continuous chain of my ancestors' connection to the soil of Afghanistan was, for the first time, broken. The implications of this would manifest throughout all our lives. Secondly, we were crossing a historically controversial line—the Durand Line—drawn in 1893 as part of the Great Game. It was a line that for most of its history had been considered illegitimate by Afghanistan. When Pakistan was formed in 1947, the line had become the source of inherited border disputes and conflict between the two nations. The line was a symbol of the ongoing unrest created for smaller nations, forced to be recast in the image of imperial power. And yet, in a sign of the dualistic and often contradictory nature of the struggle of displaced people, it was by crossing this very line that my family sought safety.

And, thirdly, as refugees in Pakistan, we had not reached total safety. We had evaded one threat, only to be faced with another form of volatility. This time, the rejection of my family would come from the "revolutionary" Islamic identities, many of whom had fled Afghanistan during communist rule to seek safe haven in Pakistan and had flourished there. Like the communist surveillance state Afghanistan had morphed into, the different factions of the Islamist movement had eyes everywhere, with the ultimate goal of toppling the communist regime in order to rule Afghanistan. Ordinary Afghans who were now refugees in Pakistan, and who would not pledge allegiance to Islamist ideologies, were identified and accused of being, if not outright communist agents, then servants to "Western masters." An individual would be judged an "enemy of Islam" based on their belief in women's rights, or democratization of the nation, or in any form of belief that might be even slightly secular.

With this reality as the backdrop of our plight, we made our way to a refugee settlement in Peshawar. Despite the air of danger surrounding us, when I asked my mother how she felt upon reaching the camp, she said she could smell the scent of heaven there. The divine fragrance was elicited by having evaded the most immediate threats and arriving at a place where she and her young family now at least stood a chance. The ability to hope had been extended.

The "ego monsters"

A large diaspora of exiled Afghans had already settled in Peshawar, many of them waiting for papers to arrive from various foreign embassies who would grant them rights to resettle elsewhere. Also living in exile in Pakistan at the time was Bahaouddin Majrooh, carrying out his work at the Afghan Information Center (AIC). In addition to his journalistic credentials, Majrooh had obtained his doctorate in France and had published large bodies of work, including poetry, in French, Pashtu, and Farsi. His seminal work was an epic prose poem, "Ajhdeha-i Khudi" or "The Ego Monster," written in 1984 and still admired by many in Afghanistan and France for its layered and philosophical dimensions.

The poem follows the journey of a "midnight voyager," traversing lands with tyrannical rulers at their helms, not unlike the lands of Afghanistan and Pakistan and the men who were wrestling for their control. Through the character of the voyager, Majrooh offered his thoughts on how the nation had been disorientated by men with "unkempt beards reaching

زلمی و فریدہ ایوبی

Zelmai and Farida Ayubi

to their navels that, like black masks, covered their faces." The beards doubling as masks was Majrooh's way of acknowledging the degree to which the Islamist factions hid behind religion as a vehicle to carry out their ego-driven acts of depravity. What makes Majrooh's work empowering is that the voyager seeks answers from the refugees, asking them why they were allowing their lands, and their ancient ways, to be hijacked. In one chapter the voyager probes the refugees almost incredulously: "You welcomed the corrupt envoys of terror with open arms and allowed them to become your leaders. You accepted devilish dark beings into your midst and permitted them to further darken your ruined hearts, so that the monster can once again reside there and consume you."

For a man who, as gleaned from his writings, believed in a modus operandi that depended on not falling prey to the urges of the untamed ego, perhaps there was a recognition that, as time wore on, peoples' spirits would also wear down and become increasingly vulnerable to the whims of tyranny. They would be trapped in the web of greed and violence being spun around them. Majrooh understood the need to end the conflict as quickly as possible to avoid this relinquishment of the nation's spirit.

By 1987 there were whispers of an imminent Soviet withdrawal from Afghanistan and many, including in the international community, were beginning to look at different endgame scenarios for the nation. Majrooh and the AIC broke their usually apolitical reporting stance. Majrooh recognized that the Soviet withdrawal was a watershed moment—the moment that would determine how the nation moved forward. There were many vying for the leadership; among them, the leaders of the various Islamist factions. But Majrooh argued that they, just like the communist rulers in the nation, would not be accepted as legitimate by the people because of the disorderly means by which their ascension was unfolding. In addition, Majrooh argued that there would always be alternative mujahideen groups that would find the justification to challenge the central government, leading to ongoing unrest.

There were, meanwhile, murmurings of a groundswell of support for the return of the last king, Zahir Shah, from his exile in Italy. Many, including Majrooh, perceived him to be a symbol of legitimacy, untainted by the past decade of corruption and cruelty that had been seared into the national psyche. And, although the return of Zahir Shah as a figurehead was regarded as a potential solution, it was under the proviso that he would not return as the head of a monarchy, but as the interim leader of a transitional democratic government.

In order to investigate, in some quantitative way, the degree of support for the return of Zahir Shah, Majrooh and the AIC organized for a survey of Afghan refugees in the camps across Pakistan from January to July 1987, asking their opinion on what they would like to see take place after Soviet withdrawal. In the publication of the report in the AIC's July 1987 edition,

Bahaouddin Majrooh and wife Khalidah Majrooh

Majrooh acknowledged upfront the limitations of the survey, including that not all the camps had been surveyed and that it was harder to speak to women than to men. Nonetheless, the sample size and consistency of responses were large enough to provide telling results.

Of the more than 2000 respondents from 106 of the 249 refugee camps, representing all major ethno-linguistic groups and all political leanings, 72 percent wanted to see the return of Zahir Shah as the national leader. Less than half of one percent wanted to see any of the Islamist leaders take control of the nation. In response, Zahir Shah broke his silence, broadcasting on the BBC World Service that he would return to serve his people, if that was what his people desired, and that under no circumstances would he seek to restore a monarchy.

The survey of Afghan refugees had crystallized what many had long assumed about the existence of support for Zahir Shah; it confirmed there was a political solution to the crisis that offered a chance to restore the country's fading pulse. Furthermore, the United Nations Commission on Human Rights had been meeting with Majrooh and referencing his survey in its propositions for peace. Just like the grandfather he shared with my mother, Sufi intermediary Pachah Sahib Tigiri, Majrooh was as neutral a force as possible. Unlike many others, particularly those now vying for control, he had remained untainted by corrupt politics and unseduced by the lure of the personal power so readily accrued during times of instability. He was thus positioned, and regarded, as the best person to broker the UN-driven mediations for peace in a manner that reflected the wishes of the overwhelming majority of Afghanistan's people.

But it was for exactly these same reasons that Majrooh constituted a serious threat to the radical Islamic parties and their plans for takeover after the Soviet departure. Among the most vocal in opposition to the return of the last king was Gulbuddin Hekmatyar, of Hizb-i Islami. Hekmatyar accused Zahir Shah of being unfit to lead the nation because he had abandoned it to be in the West and had made no sacrifices for Afghanistan. It is not difficult to understand how these self-proclaimed leaders would have felt deeply threatened by the man whose dignified and theoretically achievable plan for peace in the nation eradicated the Islamist parties' need to exist. Majrooh was indirectly exposing them as the "ego monster" frauds they were and, for this, he would pay dearly.

On 11 February 1988, on the eve of his sixtieth birthday, there was a knock at Majrooh's door. He answered, and was met with shots fired from a rifle at point-blank range. His death was a blow to all who knew him, and to the nation. No one ever claimed responsibility for his murder or was held to account, but many believe it was carried out on the orders of Hekmatyar. Majrooh would certainly have understood that he was on a perilous collision course with those whose legitimacy he was challenging, but he had persisted nonetheless.

The history of Afghanistan brims, no doubt, with heroes like Majrooh, many of whom will remain unknown forever. But, even if they are nameless and faceless, perhaps the most important thing to know about them is what they were bound to—a belief in something that outweighed the gravity, and transcended the depravity, of the rife lawlessness that was engulfing their world. For them, it was easier to draw their last breath than to welcome corrupt envoys into their hearts. Many Afghan people would be asked to navigate this dichotomy in their own way.

Transitions

After just days in Pakistan, my father was again receiving threats to his life, this time for refusing to subscribe to the ideologies of the numerous warring Islamist factions. The little money we had, raised by managing to secure a quarter of the funds from the sale of our house in Kabul (the rest of which went to the "people's" communist state), had gradually been extorted. The threats escalated and would become increasingly real. Someone followed my father to the makeshift tent my family called home and informed him that, unless he paid a bribe, he would be listed as a communist and killed. Such was the punishment for refusing to take on this emerging and extremist form of Islam. But it had all played out once before—these were the same bullish and existential threats we had faced from the communist regime in Afghanistan, only this time from those who claimed to be its antithesis. It was the next tipping point, signalling that it was time, yet again, for us to leave.

Our trajectory to Australia began via the kindness and selflessness of a family friend, Dr Nouria Salehi; our connections extended back generations. She had completed her PhD in nuclear medicine in France and, between various teaching stints at the University of Kabul, traveled back to Europe to study and work. By 1981 she had moved to Australia and was working at the Royal Melbourne Hospital, while supporting the resettlement of Afghan families to Australia. A humanitarian with many links to the community, both in Afghanistan and Australia, her work has been recognized on many levels, and among her accolades is her membership of the Order of Australia. By chance, my father saw Dr Salehi's father in Peshawar just as he was preparing to leave for Australia. He asked my father to write down everyone's names and dates of birth for him to pass on to Nouria, who would organize to sponsor our family, as she had many other Afghan families.

The paperwork was lodged, and we began the wait for a decision from the officials at the Australian Embassy in Pakistan. There were clouds of paranoia and danger hanging in the air, so the plans to leave the country had to be made quietly. Once a week, in the early hours of the morning so he wasn't seen, my father would make his way over to the embassy quarter.

Every week, for months, the same official would just quietly shake his head, indicating that nothing had yet come through. On one visit he called my father over to tell him that there was an issue with our application, which was why it was taking so long to process, and that this probably meant we would be rejected.

Undeterred, once a week, every week, my father would show up at his office. One day the official called him over and smiled. My father said he knew this was his day for good news. Against many odds, we had been accepted as migrants to Australia.

Life in Australia

In 1987, when we arrived in Australia, life was bathed in a warm glow and with the ethereal scent of safety. We were among the few who had left Afghanistan with their family still intact. We had escaped with our lives, and with the opportunity to live in a setting free from the specter of war and the scrambling of the human spirit that it creates. But attached to this opportunity were the shadows of all that had been lost.

The disconnection from the ancestral lands upon which generations of my family's history had unfolded, and which were firmly imprinted on our auras, would come to define the trajectory of our lives. Stripped bare of all that was known and familiar, those lives would now unfold in a setting that was, in some ways, disorientating. As displaced people, the quest we now faced was to find a way of reconciling back to its rightful "oneness," the seeming binary of joy and sorrow, or risk being lost in the void in between.

For our first two years in Australia we lived in Melbourne's St Kilda, in a small, rented two-bedroom apartment, before we moved to Adelaide in 1989. There was an innocent simplicity in attempting to negotiate the norms of everyday life. My parents had arrived with a basic grasp of English and soon placed themselves in state-funded language classes for migrants and refugees. My sisters were all enrolled in school. Our daily routine was a walk to drop off my sisters to their classes as I watched longingly from my stroller, wishing I could join them. My parents and I would carry on, and they would drop me off at childcare and catch the tram into town for their English classes. In an environment where much of their skill-set from Afghanistan was rendered obsolete, they would spend years in menial jobs, trying to make ends meet for their young family.

In 1994 my youngest sister, Raihanah, was born in Adelaide—the only one of the five of us born in Australia. My sisters and I had spent our formative years in Australia with a common hunger to learn, our imaginations cultivated through reading almost every children's book in our local library. We were connected to one another—and always, in some way, to the history that preceded us. Our strongest links to our ancestry were through language and food. We had all been raised with Farsi as our first language, and food was the recurring centerpiece around which we would all gather, celebrating birthdays or inviting people for mehmanis—gatherings during which the long-cultivated spirit of Afghan hospitality would shine. Part of the ritual of these occasions was to prepare the food together. Whether we were folding mantu, making bolani, or rolling kofta, we would do so communally, in an act of connection and bonding that preceded sitting together to eat.

For us, as children, food was embedded as one of the few tangible associations keeping us tethered to, and a part of, the layers of Afghanistan's spiritual and cultural dimensions. For my parents, food took on a new poignancy, as an evoker of memories conjuring the otherwise fleeting reality of their past. For my mother in particular, cooking was a means to keep alive, and pass on, the ancient ways that had been honored and cultivated along her own maternal lineage. She knew she was the keeper of an old art that was, in the realities of the modern world, being scattered into near oblivion, exiled as part of the several ongoing decades of conflict in Afghanistan. She would tell us that it was treasure she was keeping—and she was keeping it to pass on to us.

Another connection to our history came in the form of the challenges it created. The arc of displacement inevitably bent towards questions of identity and belonging. There were facets of life in Australia that collided with Afghanistan's cultural norms and, as we grew into young adults, we would have to muster the courage and strength to negotiate our paths between these competing expectations, while also creating space for the expression of our newly emerging selves.

Defiant in spirit, we were defined in our own ways by an awareness of being the first to tread this new terrain—physically, spiritually, and intellectually. The call upon us was to remove from our path ahead the boulders of expectation—from both our cultural worlds—that were at odds with, and would sink, the human spirit. Our life story was one in which we had the chance to not be confined by the trajectory of increasing violence that was unfolding in Afghanistan and, if not consciously, then subconsciously at least, we understood the value of this gift and our responsibility to grow our wings, for ourselves and for generations to come. We would not be defined by the corrosive aspects of tradition, which should have either never existed or long been abandoned, and, equally, we would not erase our differences in order to be the same as others—often the price of the ticket of inclusion. We had to overcome these unnatural demands and, instead, become a version of ourselves that was at once broader and deeper.

Our trials and tribulations reached in and extracted some of our deeper truths, the boons of our journey. We learned that we needed one another—we were our only constant in this trajectory of displacement. The relationship between us children and our parents had become one of reciprocity, where the differences in the lenses through which we saw the world would bring into focus a sharper picture moving forward. We had learned that all that was seemingly solid could vaporise overnight into thin air. And that defining oneself by the sense of prestige that accompanies the acquisition of land, cultural hierarchies, or material goods was ultimately illusory. When pressed in the face of adversity, the thing that matters most is the chance to experience life in a way that does not forcibly demand conformity. We had learned that the most durable and sustainable way to live was in recognition of the very human tendency to be flawed. Any ideology claiming absolute knowledge—such as the systems of communism and of fundamental Islam that had gripped Afghanistan—was using its own utopian guise to unleash a dehumanizing oppression.

We had learned that the supposedly irreconcilable binaries into which many realities of our present world are split—such as those of East and West—are two sides of the same coin, waiting to be reconciled into their singular human form.

The butterfly effect

These lessons were beckoning us to transfigure into a version of ourselves that would have something life-giving to offer both ourselves and those around us. In 2009 we opened the doors to Parwana. Fittingly for our own metamorphosis, the word parwana is Farsi for "butterfly." It was a quiet start; there were no grand plans, other than to see if people liked the food. But it was important to us, because it was a manifestation of all the things we had learned on our journey of displacement.

Parwana is underpinned by my mother's vision— her belief that through her knowledge of the art of Afghan food, gifted to her from her mother and her foremothers, she had been entrusted with a treasure of old, a symbol of Afghanistan's monumental and culturally interwoven past. This ancient gift was all the more priceless because it captured the essence of the lives lost and the dreams dissipated during the course of our journey. Parwana had come to be our recognition and expression of the inseparability of joy and sorrow. The many tears of loss had stripped us bare and raw and ready to create something in an image that was not confined by dispiriting boundaries of fear and false binaries, but in acknowledgment of what it was to be imperfectly and joyously human. Parwana was an ode to our past, buoyed by the hopes of our future.

The recipes in this chapter include some that have come to be favorites at Parwana. They are offered in the spirit of sharing as widely as possible the treasure my mother has been keeping. They are shared in recognition of the act of reconciling grief and joy.

BANJAAN BORANI

بادنجان بورانی

Sunflower oil for deep-frying,
  plus ½ cup (125 ml) extra
2 eggplants, peeled and halved lengthways
1 large yellow onion, sliced into
  semicircles
6 garlic cloves, coarsely chopped
2 moderately hot fresh red chilies,
  thinly sliced
2 teaspoons ground coriander
1 teaspoon white sugar
1 teaspoon ground turmeric
1 teaspoon ground red pepper
2 teaspoons white vinegar
5 large tomatoes, sliced
½ cup (125 ml) boiling water
Fresh mint and ground red pepper, to serve
Salt

FOR THE YOGURT DRESSING
2 cups (1 lb 2 oz/500 g) Greek yogurt
1 garlic clove, crushed

Banjaan borani has become a signature dish at Parwana. Its popularity arises perhaps from the overall balance of textures and flavors—soft, melt-in-the-mouth eggplant, simmered in a slightly acidic tomato base, topped with a tangy, cooling yogurt dressing. My mother recalls that in Afghanistan, banjaan borani was a favorite during the summer, when eggplants were in peak season.

That this dish has endured to become a favorite in Australia, speaks to the resonance of the human spirit across seemingly disparate worlds, and to the constantly evolving nature of culture.

The recipe below is how banjaan borani would be prepared at home, to eat alongside challaw (see page 111) or another rice dish.

In a large saucepan, heat enough oil for deep-frying to 325°F (170°C) on an oil thermometer.

Gently add eggplant pieces, without overcrowding the pan, and fry, flipping them over occasionally, until they are golden on both sides and soft all the way through. Set aside in a colander placed over a bowl to catch the excess oil and repeat with the remaining eggplant pieces.

Heat the extra oil in a large frying pan over high heat and fry the onion, garlic, and fresh chilies, stirring constantly, for 2 minutes, or until fragrant. Reduce the heat to low and add the coriander, sugar, turmeric, ground red pepper, vinegar, and 1 tablespoon salt, stirring for 2 minutes, for the flavors to combine.

Arrange the tomato slices over this base to cover, then add the boiling water. Gently layer the eggplants on top using tongs and increase the heat to high. Bring to a boil, then reduce the heat to low, cover the pan, and simmer for 10 minutes.

Meanwhile, to make the yogurt dressing, mix the yogurt, garlic, and ½ teaspoon salt in a bowl to combine well.

Spread half the yogurt dressing over a large serving platter then, using a flat spoon, gently lift out the eggplant pieces and arrange them over the yogurt, without overlapping. Spoon the onion and tomato sauce over the eggplants and decoratively dollop or spread the remaining yogurt dressing on top. Garnish with mint leaves and red pepper, and serve hot.

DAHL

دال

2 cups (14½ oz/410 g) red split lentils
½ cup (125 ml) sunflower oil
2 yellow onions, finely diced
2 garlic cloves, finely chopped
1 moderately hot fresh red chili,
   thinly sliced
4 large tomatoes, diced
1 teaspoon ground turmeric
1 teaspoon ground coriander
1 teaspoon curry powder
½ teaspoon chaar masalah (see page 21)
Chopped fresh cilantro, to serve
Salt

Common throughout Afghanistan and across the subcontinent, dahl is an easy dish to vary—be it in the type of lentils, the spices, or the amount of chili used. We serve dahl at Parwana, and this recipe uses red split lentils for a soft and creamy texture, perfect to eat alongside challaw (see page 111) or a palaw rice dish (see pages 113, 114, 125, 126, and 129), or simply with some naan flatbread (see page 82).

Add the lentils and 6 cups (1.5 liters) water to a pot, bring to a boil, then reduce the heat to low and simmer for 15 minutes, or until the lentils are softened. Drain in a colander, discarding the water, and set aside in the pot.

In a separate pot, heat the oil over high heat and fry the onions for 5 minutes, or until they are golden brown. Add the garlic and chili and fry for a further 2 minutes, or until softened and fragrant. Add the tomatoes and cook, stirring occasionally, for 2–3 minutes, or until softened. Stir in the spices and 1 tablespoon salt and cook for a further 2 minutes, or until fragrant.

Add the lentils and 4¼ cups (1 liter) water to the pot and bring to a boil. Cook for 5–8 minutes, or until the dahl has thickened and absorbed all the flavors in the sauce. To serve, ladle the dahl into a serving bowl and garnish with fresh cilantro.

FASOOLIA

فاشلیه

1 cup (250 ml) sunflower oil
1 large yellow onion, very finely diced
Heaped 1 tablespoon grated garlic
Heaped 1 tablespoon grated fresh ginger
1 teaspoon ground turmeric
1 teaspoon ground red pepper
1 teaspoon ground coriander
1 teaspoon ground cumin
2 teaspoons chaar masalah (see page 21)
6 large tomatoes, puréed in a blender
1 cup (9 oz/250 g) plain yogurt
2¼ lb (1 kg) green beans, trimmed
  and halved
Salt

Fasoolia is a sautéed green bean dish with variations in the cuisines of countries along the Silk Road, from Afghanistan to the Middle East and the Mediterranean. In this recipe, the beans are cooked in a tomato and onion sauce leaving them velvety and tender, but not overly soft. Fasoolia is usually enjoyed with challaw (see page 111) or a palaw rice dish (see pages 113, 114, 125, 126, and 129) and some yogurt, or simply with naan flatbread (see page 82) to mop up all the delicious sauce.

Heat the oil in a medium pot over high heat and fry the onion, garlic, and ginger for 5 minutes, or until the onion is golden. Reduce the heat to medium, add all the spices and 1 tablespoon salt (or to taste), and sauté for 2 minutes, or until fragrant. Add the tomatoes and yogurt, and stir continuously until the sauce begins to boil. Reduce the heat to low and simmer gently for 10 minutes, or until the sauce thickens and deepens in color.

Meanwhile, bring 8½ cups (2 liters) water and 1 tablespoon salt to a boil. Add the beans and boil for 5 minutes, or until they are bright green and tender-crisp. Drain in a colander, discarding the water. Add the beans to the sauce and cook for 4 minutes, so they absorb the flavors. Serve fasoolia hot in a decorative bowl.

BAAMIYAH

باميه

1 lb 5 oz (600 g) okra, trimmed
1½ cups (375 ml) sunflower oil for
   frying, plus 1 tablespoon extra
2 moderately hot fresh red chilies,
   thinly sliced
5 garlic cloves, finely chopped
2 large tomatoes, diced
1 tablespoon lemon juice,
½ teaspoon white sugar
1 teaspoon ground coriander
Salt

Okra is a summer vegetable in Afghanistan, grown throughout the countryside, including in my family's province of Laghman. On hot afternoons before dinner, baamiyah, an okra dish, would be eaten alongside a cooling glass of dogh (see page 195).

Here, okra didn't used to be as widely available as it is now, and so on the occasions we had it at home, it always evoked memories of baamiyah cooked on summer days in Afghanistan.

Halve each okra horizontally through the middle, then wash and pat dry with paper towels.

Heat the oil for frying in a frying pan over high heat to 350°F (180°C) on an oil thermometer. Fry the okra in batches, so as to not overcrowd the pan, stirring gently to ensure they are fried evenly, for 5 minutes, or until golden. Set aside on a plate.

Heat the extra oil in a saucepan over high heat and fry the chili and garlic for 2 minutes, or until softened and fragrant. Stir in the tomatoes, lemon juice, sugar, coriander, and 1 teaspoon salt, then add the okra, and mix gently to combine.

Sauté the ingredients for 5 minutes, then reduce the heat to low and cook for a further 10 minutes, or until the okra is completely cooked through. Serve hot in a decorative bowl.

GOLPI

1 cup (250 ml) sunflower oil
1 large yellow onion, finely diced
2 garlic cloves, crushed
2 teaspoons curry powder
1 teaspoon chaar masalah (see page 21)
1 teaspoon white sugar
3 dried bay leaves
4 large tomatoes, puréed in a blender
1 tablespoon white vinegar
1 cup (250 ml) boiling water
1 small cauliflower, broken into florets,
  large florets torn apart
Salt

Golpi is a curried cauliflower dish. My mother recalls that, in Afghanistan, cauliflowers were grown throughout the provinces, as in Laghman and Jalalabad, and made typical provincial winter fare. In this recipe, the cauliflower is softened in a tomato and onion sauce and is usually eaten alongside some simple challaw rice (see page 111).

Heat the oil in a medium pot over high heat, and fry the onion and garlic for 5 minutes, or until light golden. Add the spices, sugar, bay leaves, and 1 teaspoon salt (or to taste), and cook, stirring occasionally, for 3 minutes, or until fragrant. Stir in the tomatoes and vinegar, bring to a boil, then reduce the heat to medium and simmer for 10 minutes, or until the sauce thickens and deepens in color, and oil rises to the surface.

Add the boiling water and the cauliflower to the pot and bring to a boil. Reduce the heat to medium and simmer for 15 minutes, or until the cauliflower is soft all the way through, but not mushy. Serve hot in a decorative bowl.

QORMEH KACHALOO

قورمه کچالو

¼ cup (60 ml) sunflower oil
1 large yellow onion, very finely diced
4 garlic cloves, coarsely chopped
1 teaspoon finely grated fresh ginger
1 teaspoon ground turmeric
1 teaspoon ground red pepper
1 teaspoon ground coriander
1 teaspoon ground cumin
1 teaspoon chaar masalah (see page 21)
4 large tomatoes, puréed in a blender
2½ tablespoons plain yogurt
6 medium boiling potatoes, such as red
  potatoes, each one peeled and cut
  into 6 thick wedges
1 moderately hot fresh red chili,
  thinly sliced
Salt and freshly ground black pepper

This potato curry was a staple for our family in Afghanistan, and enjoyed all year round. The potato is simmered in a tomato and yogurt sauce, giving it a soft, smooth, and creamy texture. It is a simple yet hearty and flavorsome dish. Qormeh kachaloo is usually served alongside challaw (see page 111) or a palaw rice dish (see pages 113, 114, 125, 126, and 129).

Heat the oil in a medium pot over high heat and fry the onion, garlic, and ginger for 5 minutes, until the onion is golden. Reduce the heat to medium, then add all the spices and 1 tablespoon salt (or to taste), and fry for 2 minutes, or until fragrant. Add the tomatoes and yogurt, stir continuously until the sauce begins to boil, then reduce the heat to low and simmer gently for 10 minutes, or until the sauce thickens and deepens in color.

Add the potatoes to the pot and cook over high heat for 5 minutes, to heat the potatoes through, then reduce the heat to medium-low. Simmer for 20–25 minutes, or until the potatoes absorb the flavors of the sauce and are soft when pierced, but still retain their shape. Serve hot, garnished with fresh chili and black pepper.

◆ ◆

KADOO BORANI

¼ cup (60 ml) sunflower oil, plus
  1 tablespoon extra
1 lb 2 oz (500 g) pumpkin or winter
  squash, such as kabocha or acorn,
  peeled and cut roughly into 1½ in
  (4 cm) cubes
1 large yellow onion, thinly sliced
4 garlic cloves, coarsely chopped
1-2 moderately hot fresh red chilies,
  sliced lengthways
1 teaspoon ground turmeric
2 tomatoes, sliced into rings
1 teaspoon dried mint
Salt

FOR THE YOGURT DRESSING
1 cup (9 oz/250 g) Greek-style yogurt
1 garlic clove, crushed

Kadoo borani is a pumpkin dish served with a yogurt dressing. It's similar in style to the eggplant dish of banjaan borani (see page 169), with the word "borani" referring to any braised vegetable served with yogurt. The other flavors in this dish, such as the zing of garlic and the sweetness of slightly caramelized onions, draw complementary flavors out of the pumpkin, resulting in a dish with layers of texture and flavor.

This dish originated in the eastern provinces of Afghanistan, where my family is from, and was something my mother loved to make. Today, kadoo borani has endured as a favorite in our household, where we eat it with naan flatbread (see page 82) to mop up the yogurt infused with the flavors of the pumpkin and sauce.

Heat the oil in a frying pan over high heat and fry the pumpkin, turning occasionally, for 6–8 minutes, or until golden all over. Remove from the pan and set aside on a plate.

Clean the pan of the excess oil and return it to high heat. Add the extra oil and fry the onion, garlic, and chilies, stirring occasionally, for 3–4 minutes, or until the onion has softened and caramelized. Add the turmeric and 1 teaspoon salt, and mix to combine. Spread the mixture evenly over the base of the pan and arrange the tomato slices on top. Layer the pumpkin over the tomatoes, cover the pan with a lid, and cook, gently shaking the pan back and forth occasionally to prevent sticking, for 10 minutes, or until the tomato and onion base is cooked and the flavors have infused the pumpkin.

Meanwhile, to make the yogurt dressing, whisk the yogurt, garlic, and ½ teaspoon salt in a bowl until smooth.

Spread half the yogurt dressing over the base of your serving dish with the back of a serving spoon. Arrange the pumpkin, and onion and tomato mixture over the yogurt. Decoratively drizzle or spoon the remaining yogurt dressing on top and serve hot, sprinkled with dried mint.

NAKHOT
نخود

2 cups (14 oz/400 g) dried chickpeas
1 cup (250 ml) sunflower oil
1 large yellow onion, finely diced
2 garlic cloves, crushed
2 teaspoons curry powder
1 teaspoon chaar masalah (see page 21)
1 teaspoon white sugar
3 dried bay leaves
4 large tomatoes, puréed in a blender
1 tablespoon white vinegar
1 cup (250 ml) boiling water
Fresh parsley leaves, coarsely chopped,
  to serve
Salt

Legumes are a key component in Afghan cuisine and they are widely cultivated in the country. This is a simple, rustic chickpea curry that is enjoyed throughout Afghanistan with challaw (see page 111), a palaw rice dish (see pages 113, 114, 125, 126, and 129), or naan flatbread (see page 82).

Start this recipe a day ahead to soak the chickpeas.

To soak the chickpeas, cover them with at least 2 in (5 cm) cold water in a bowl and set aside for at least 8 hours. The chickpeas will expand as they soak up the water, so you will need a bowl large enough to accommodate this.

Heat the oil in a medium pot over high heat and fry the onion and garlic for 3–4 minutes, or until light golden. Add the spices, sugar, bay leaves, and 1 teaspoon salt (or to taste), and cook, stirring occasionally, for 3 minutes, or until fragrant. Stir in the tomatoes and vinegar, bring to a boil, then reduce the heat to medium and simmer for 10 minutes, or until the sauce thickens and deepens in color, and the oil rises to the surface. Add the boiling water to the sauce and stir to combine. Increase the heat to high and bring to a boil. Cook for 3 minutes, or until the sauce thickens slightly again.

Drain the chickpeas, rinse in cold water, and drain again. Add the chickpeas and 8½ cups (2 liters) cold water to a medium pot, and bring to a boil. Reduce the heat to medium, cover with a lid, and cook for 35 minutes, or until they have softened, but still retain their shape.

Drain the chickpeas in a colander, discarding the water, then add them to the sauce and simmer over medium heat for 5 minutes, to heat through and to absorb the flavors of the sauce.

Sprinkle with parsley and serve alongside your preferred rice dish or simply with some naan.

QORMEH GOSFAND

قورمه گوسفند

½ cup (3¾ oz/105 g) dried plums
   (available from Afghan or Persian
   grocery shops)
1 cup (250 ml) sunflower oil
1 large yellow onion, very finely diced
Heaped 1 tablespoon finely grated garlic
Heaped 1 tablespoon finely grated ginger
2 teaspoons ground turmeric
1 teaspoon ground red pepper
1 teaspoon ground coriander
1 teaspoon ground cumin
2 teaspoons chaar masalah (see page 21)
6 large tomatoes, puréed in a blender
1 cup (9 oz/250 g) plain yogurt
2¼ lb (1 kg) bone-in lamb shoulder, cut
   into large chunks
2 boiling potatoes, such as red or Yukon
   gold, peeled and cut into large wedges
Thinly sliced green chili, to garnish
Salt

This lamb curry is a staple dish of Afghan cuisine, and a favorite at Parwana. The lamb pieces are cooked soft and tender, absorbing the flavors of the sauce in which they simmer. It is traditionally served with a rice dish or naan bread, or atop sholeh Ghorbandi (see page 120).

◆

In a pot, boil the dried plums in 3 cups (750 ml) water for 10 minutes, or until the plums soften. Set aside.

Heat the oil in a pot over high heat and fry the onion, garlic, and ginger for 3–4 minutes, or until the onion is light golden. Reduce the heat to medium, add half of the turmeric, along with all the rest of the spices and 1 tablespoon salt (or to taste), and fry, stirring occasionally, for 2 minutes for the flavors to combine. Add the tomatoes and yogurt and stir continuously until the sauce begins to boil; it's important to keep stirring until it has reached boiling point, otherwise the yogurt will split.

Reduce the heat to low and simmer gently for 12 minutes, or until the sauce thickens and deepens in color.

Put the potatoes and 4¼ cups (1 liter) water into a medium pot. Add the remaining turmeric and 2 teaspoons salt, then boil for 5 minutes, or until tender when pierced with the tip of a knife. Drain the potatoes in a colander, discarding the water, and set aside.

Place the lamb, 1 cup (250 ml) water, and 2 teaspoons salt in a pressure cooker, seal the lid, and cook for 15 minutes. Remove the lamb and add to the sauce. Stir in the potatoes and plums with their cooking liquid, and simmer gently over low heat for 10 minutes, or until the sauce thickens again, and the meat absorbs the flavor of the sauce. Serve in a bowl, garnished with green chili.

QORMEH MORGH

In Afghanistan, poultry wasn't as readily available as red meat, so this chicken curry was not prepared as often as something like a lamb curry. This dish is almost always eaten alongside challaw (see page 111) or a palaw rice dish (see pages 114, 125, and 126), with naan breads (see pages 82–83) on the side.

2¼ lb (1 kg) whole chicken, skin removed, cut into joints
1 cup (250 ml) sunflower oil
1 large yellow onion, finely diced
2 garlic cloves, crushed
2 teaspoons curry powder
1 teaspoon chaar masalah (see page 21)
1 teaspoon white sugar
3 dried bay leaves
4 large tomatoes, puréed in a blender
1 tablespoon white vinegar
3 cups (750 ml) boiling water
2½ tablespoons yellow split peas
Salt

Place the chicken in a medium pot with 12 cups (3 liters) water and 1 tablespoon salt. Bring to a boil and cook the chicken for 15–20 minutes, or until the pieces are half-cooked and have lost their pink rawness. Drain in a colander, discarding the water, and set the chicken aside while you prepare the sauce.

Heat the oil in a medium pot over high heat and fry the onion and garlic for 3–4 minutes, or until they are light golden and fragrant. Add the spices, sugar, bay leaves, and 1 teaspoon salt, and fry, stirring occasionally, for 3 minutes, or until fragrant and combined. Stir in the tomatoes and vinegar, bring to a boil, then reduce the heat to medium and simmer for 5–6 minutes, or until the sauce thickens and deepens in color, and oil rises to the surface. Add 1 cup (250 ml) of the boiling water and increase the heat to high. Bring to a boil and cook for 3 minutes, or until the sauce thickens slightly again.

Add the chicken to the sauce and cook for about 15 minutes, or until the chicken is completely cooked through, has absorbed the flavors of the sauce, and the sauce thickens further.

While the chicken is cooking, boil the split peas in the remaining boiling water in a small pot for 8–10 minutes, or until they are soft but still retain their shape. Drain and scatter over the qormeh morgh.

LOBEYAH

لوبیا

2 cups (13 oz/360 g) dried red
 kidney beans
1 cup (250 ml) sunflower oil
1 large yellow onion, very finely diced
Heaped 1 tablespoon finely grated garlic
Heaped 1 tablespoon finely grated ginger
1 teaspoon ground turmeric
1 teaspoon ground red pepper
1 teaspoon ground coriander
1 teaspoon ground cumin
2 teaspoons chaar masalah (see page 21)
6 large tomatoes, puréed in a blender
1 cup (9 oz/250 g) plain yogurt
Salt

Like chickpeas, red kidney beans are a staple of the Afghan diet and, as well as in this curry, they're cooked in various ways, including in sauces used to dress dumplings or in soups. Start this recipe a day ahead to soak the kidney beans. Serve with your favorite rice dish, naan, and accompaniments of choice.

Cover the kidney beans with at least 2 in (5 cm) cold water in a bowl and set aside for at least 8 hours. The beans will expand as they soak up the water, so you will need a bowl large enough to accommodate this.

Heat the oil in a large saucepan over high heat and fry the onion, garlic, and ginger for 3–4 minutes, or until the onion is light golden. Reduce the heat to medium, add all the spices and 1 tablespoon salt (or to taste), and fry, stirring occasionally, for 2 minutes for the flavors to combine. Add the tomatoes and yogurt, and stir continuously until the sauce begins to boil; it's important to keep stirring until it has reached boiling point, otherwise the yogurt will split. Reduce the heat to low and simmer gently for 10–12 minutes, or until the sauce has thickened and is rich in color.

Drain the kidney beans, and rinse them in cold water. Add the beans and 8½ cups (2 liters) cold water to a medium pot, bring to a boil, then reduce the heat to medium. Cover with a lid and cook for 35 minutes, or until the beans are soft, but still retain their shape.

Drain in a colander, discarding the water, then add the beans to the sauce and simmer over medium heat for a further 5 minutes to heat through and absorb the flavors of the sauce.

SAMAROQ

سمارق

½ cup (125 ml) sunflower oil
4 garlic cloves, thinly sliced
2 moderately hot fresh red chilies,
 thinly sliced
1 red onion, finely diced
2 large tomatoes, diced
3 lb 5 oz (1.5 kg) mixed mushrooms, such
 as cremini and button mushrooms, or any
 varieties you prefer, evenly sliced
1 teaspoon chaar masalah (see page 21)
Fresh curry leaves, to garnish (optional)
Salt

During the time my parents were living in Afghanistan, mushrooms were in abundance at the start of spring. Foraged varieties were fleshy and thick-stemmed, and took a while to cook. Using the knowledge held by locals, poisonous ones were carefully avoided.

This mixed mushroom curry, sautéed in garlic, onion, and traditional spices, is best enjoyed with your favorite rice dish or naan bread.

Heat the oil in a large saucepan over high heat and sauté the garlic and chilies for 1–2 minutes to soften. Add the onion and fry for 3–4 minutes, or until golden brown. Stir in the tomatoes and 1 tablespoon salt, and cook until the tomatoes break down and a sauce forms.

Add the mushrooms to the sauce and cook, stirring occasionally, for 10 minutes; the mushrooms will release a lot of liquid, but continue cooking them until the liquid evaporates. Add the chaar masalah and stir it into the mushrooms and sauce, then serve the samaroq hot, garnished with fresh curry leaves, with rice or naan on the side.

Traditional Afghan dress; opposite: Samaroq (page 187)

BARTAH

4 eggplants
Sunflower oil for deep-frying
1 garlic clove, finely crushed
¼ cup (60 ml) lemon juice
1 moderately hot fresh red chili, finely
  chopped, plus extra, thinly sliced,
  to serve
Small handful of fresh mint leaves,
  finely chopped
Olive oil for drizzling
Salt

This smoked eggplant dip is one of a trio of dips served at Parwana. During the height of eggplant season in Afghanistan, my mother recalls excess eggplants being made into bartah to ensure they did not go to waste. It is usually served with naan breads (see pages 82 and 83).

To make the dip, the eggplants are roasted over an open flame, but if you don't have a gas stove, grill them over the flames of a barbecue or even under the broiler.

Roast 2 eggplants with the skin on directly over the flames of a gas stove top or barbecue, turning occasionally, until they are soft and the skin is charred all over. This gives the dip its deeply smoky taste. Set the eggplants aside to cool, then cut them in half, scoop out the flesh, discarding the peel, and place it in a bowl.

In a large saucepan, heat enough oil for deep-frying to 325°F (170°C) on an oil thermometer. Peel and slice the remaining 2 eggplants and deep-fry, turning occasionally, for 2–3 minutes each side, or until golden on both sides and soft all the way through. Remove the eggplant slices from the oil using tongs or a slotted spoon, add them to the smoked eggplant, and mash with a fork to a slightly chunky consistency.

Add the garlic, lemon juice, chili, mint leaves, and 1½ teaspoons salt, and mix to combine thoroughly. Transfer to a serving bowl, then drizzle with olive oil. Decorate with the extra chili slices.

JAAN-E-AMA

جان عمه

This yogurt and cucumber dip is served as an accompaniment to many Afghan dishes and is much like the tzatziki of Mediterranean cuisine. It is served at Parwana, with the yogurt acting to cool and balance the heat of the dishes with which it's served.

2 English cucumbers
4 cups (2¼ lb/1 kg) Greek-style yogurt or homemade yogurt (see page 26)
1 garlic clove, crushed
2 teaspoons dried mint
Heaped 1 tablespoon coarsely chopped fresh mint leaves, plus extra leaves to garnish
Salt

Peel and grate the cucumbers into a bowl, then squeeze out the excess moisture over the sink with your hands. Return the cucumber to the bowl with the yogurt, garlic, dried mint, and 1 teaspoon salt (or to taste), and mix vigorously to combine.

Serve in a decorative bowl, garnished with the fresh mint leaves, as an accompaniment to any Afghan meal.

From left to right:
Bartah (page 190);
Jaan-e-ama (page 191)

DOGH

3⅔ cups (2 lb/910 g) plain yogurt
2 cups (500 ml) chilled water
½ English cucumber, finely diced
2½ tablespoons fresh mint leaves,
  finely chopped
Ice cubes, to serve
Salt

Dogh is a cooling, savory yogurt and cucumber drink that is traditionally enjoyed with meals on hot summer days in Afghanistan. Like the many variations of lassi across the subcontinent, these savory (and sometimes sweet) yogurt-based drinks are a staple of the country's cuisine, enjoyed for their digestive properties and because they are mildly sleep-inducing.

Have some water in the fridge chilled and ready to make dogh.

Whisk the yogurt with the chilled water and salt to taste in a large bowl until well combined and frothy. Stir in the cucumber and mint, then pour the dogh into a large jug and add ice cubes. Serve in individual glasses.

SHIR YAKHEH GULAB

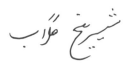

4¼ cups (1 liter) heavy whipping cream
2 cups (500 ml) condensed milk
1 teaspoon pandan food coloring,
* or any green food coloring*
1 teaspoon cardamom pods, crushed
* with a mortar and pestle*
1 tablespoon rosewater
½ cup (2½ oz/70 g) crushed pistachios
Slivered pistachios and rose petals,
* to serve*

Shir yakh is a type of traditional ice cream. In Afghanistan, during the hot summer months, ice-cream shops, called shir yakh feroshees, or street vendors with carts, would sell an assortment of ice creams and other cold desserts. My sister Fatema remembers going into beautiful little shops after school to buy shir yakh; they were colorful and decoratively tiled and had Bollywood music playing in the background.

This shir yakh, with rose and pistachios, is a favorite at Parwana.

Process the cream, condensed milk, and food coloring in a food processor for 3–4 minutes, or until stiff peaks form.

Transfer the mixture to a clean bowl and add the cardamom, rosewater, and pistachios. Fold through gently to combine well, then transfer to a large airtight container.

Cover the entire surface of the ice cream directly with plastic wrap to avoid ice crystals forming. Cover the container with a lid and freeze for at least 10 hours before serving, scattered with slivered pistachios and rose petals.

SHIR YAKHEH ZANJAFIL

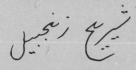

Like the rose and pistachio ice cream on page 196, this homemade ginger and walnut ice cream is a firm favorite at Parwana.

4¼ cups (1 liter) heavy whipping cream
2 cups (500 ml) condensed milk
Heaped 1 tablespoon cooking caramel
    (available from supermarkets and Asian
    grocery shops)
2½ tablespoons ground ginger
½ cup (2 oz/60 g) coarsely chopped
    walnuts

Process the cream, condensed milk, caramel, and ginger in a food processor for 3–4 minutes, or until stiff peaks form. Transfer the mixture to a clean bowl and add the walnuts. Fold through gently to combine well, then transfer to a large airtight container.

Cover the entire surface of the ice cream directly with plastic wrap to avoid ice crystals forming. Cover the container with a lid and freeze for at least 10 hours before serving.

Chapter 5

The Movable Feast of Culture

فصل پنجم

A MIRROR TO ANCIENT TRUTHS AND CHANGING TIMES

"No one today is purely one thing … Imperialism consolidated the mixture of cultures and identities on a global scale. But its worst and most paradoxical gift was to allow people to believe that they were only, mainly, exclusively, white, or Black, or Western, or Oriental … Survival in fact is about the connections between things; in [T. S.] Eliot's phrase, reality cannot be deprived of the 'other echoes [that] inhabit the garden.'"

Edward W. Said, *Culture and Imperialism*, 1993

As my family's connection with food deepened even further with the opening of Parwana, we were realizing more and more the extent to which this embodied the means through which we could most organically relate to the world and express the influences that had come to shape our lives. Importantly, with the passing of time, the realities that set the backdrop against which our expressions unfolded were themselves changing.

This produced further layers of significance and intent behind what we were creating with Afghan cooking. If at first food was a way for us, as displaced people, to remember, commemorate, internally reconcile, and share, then over time, in a world increasingly trapped in a dominant narrative of nationalism and division, it was also about challenging, rejecting, and offering alternatives to the schisms and destruction such simplistic narratives unleashed.

The many iterations of conflict: the fall of the mujahideen and the rise of the Taliban

For Afghanistan, the global reality meant decades of ongoing fighting. The conflict in Afghanistan, which my family had left behind in 1985, continued to rage, albeit with an array of different protagonists. A year after Bahaouddin Majrooh was killed, in February 1989, the Soviets announced their withdrawal. It was the moment Majrooh had been anticipating, and preparing others for, as the opportune time for the nation to pull back together and recast itself in the image of its own people, rather than being pushed and torn apart by the dogmatic ideologies of the communists or the Islamists. But the moment passed in disarray.

After the withdrawal of the Soviet troops, the country descended deeper into civil war as the mujahideen, who had been building their resistance across the border in Pakistan, returned in an attempt to seize control of the nation. For three years after Soviet departure a Soviet puppet regime continued, but, in 1992, the communist government was eventually destabilized by the warring mujahideen factions, whose lawlessness and lust for power had intensified alongside the limitless foreign dollars and weapons pouring in from international regimes with a stake in the political outcome. Clinging to the facade of establishing a "pure" Islamic political identity in Afghanistan, but unable to decide among themselves on which of the mujahideen factions would rule the nation, they failed to create a centralized government, and drove the country further into war, based on ethnic divisions and along Shia and Sunni lines. As the divisions hardened, the party leaders—conveniently for themselves—continued to make opportunistic deals across the ethnic boundaries that they themselves had inflamed, in attempts to secure their own personal wealth and positions.

The mujahideen had begun as an earnest resistance from within tribes and communities to the oppressive, and ultimately futile, efforts of the communist regime to force Afghanistan into abandoning its own spiritual and historical aura. But now they, themselves had long adopted the mandate of the nation's oppressors, albeit in a much less organized capacity. They were also men equipped with too much ideology as a guise for their own personal ambitions, too much money and too many weapons—and ultimately it was Afghan civilians who paid the price. Atrocities were peaking across the nation; people had grown weary of the constant unpredictable chaos.

It was in such a setting that the Taliban emerged, overthrowing the dysfunctional mujahideen leaders by 1996. Their takeover was based on opposition to the ideology of the mujahideen government—

not that they felt the mujahideen had gone too far in their pursuit of religious purity, but rather they had not gone far enough. Many of the Talebs were products of a nation steeped in years of war; they had grown up in refugee camps in Pakistan and had been taught in schools alongside various international influences, unbound by the tribal, ethnic, or regional loyalties that had usually mediated Afghan society. With only a vague awareness of Afghanistan, but, once again, driven by conflated ideologies, they instituted a severe and rigid vision of life according to "true" Islamic principles. Attempting to distinguish themselves from the mujahideen, they denounced their predecessors' crimes, their seduction by foreign powers and worldly pursuits. Even without their abuses, which were particularly violating of women, the vision of the Taliban was entirely at odds with the essence of the Afghan people, who, as products of an ancient bricolage of multiethnic and multilingual roots, could not simply be reduced to, and subsumed by, a purely religious identity. The Taliban, just like the communists and the mujahideen before them, forcibly projected upon the people an ideological and depraved vision they had generated in the blinkered pressure cookers of their own experiences, rather than with the very essence of people and their needs and hopes in mind. The Afghan people wanted a way to move into the future, free from the violence generated by the waves of leaders who had trapped the country and its people in simple and violating caricatures.

Censoring culture through force

In a way, the emergence of the mujahideen, the Taliban, and the increasingly fundamentalist iterations that followed them was a sign of modernity. This was a world in which global affairs and markets were so tightly bound together that external nations could contribute to the existence of controlling powers in Afghanistan when it suited their own political and economic agendas. Their spread was made a reality when technology evolved to a point when ideas and people could move closer together and at unprecedented speeds. Even their ideologies were only possible in modernity. Traditional Afghan culture was bound to many things—familial relationships, tribal affiliations, eldership, kinship—and was expressed through arts, creativity, song, dance, celebrations, and hospitality. Religion served as just one part of

the overall balance. But now a radicalized religious ideology, fomented in the absence of traditions—which had been erased by increasingly brutal and protracted war and against a global narrative of "us versus them"—was threatening to drown out this complex and deeply historical Afghan identity.

Apart from the continued mass loss of civilian life, a huge and devastating part of the ongoing violence was the steady decline of Afghanistan's unique culture. Over the years the country's ancient artifacts and treasure troves, which had captured the world's historic millennia-long intercultural mingling, had been looted and sold for private profit. But perhaps this violation was most symbolically captured in the destruction of the giant 1500-year-old Buddhas of Bamiyan by the Taliban in March 2001, as part of a religious edict. The monumental pair, once the tallest standing Buddhas anywhere in the world and a UNESCO World Heritage Site, were carved into a Bamiyan mountain face between the third and sixth centuries, and were examples of Greco-Buddhist art and relics of the region's mixed history.

Over the centuries, the Buddha statues had been battered and weathered, but had always remained standing, even after an assault by Genghis Khan in the thirteenth century. That the statues were finally obliterated by the Taliban, to the horror and dismay of many Afghans within the country and around the world, was symbolic of how far Afghanistan had been forced from its own historical essence by those who led it. It was a sign of how far the subtleties of traditional norms and historical complexities had been diminished into a simplistic ideological narrative by the sledgehammer of fundamentalism.

Western interventions and a terrifying war on terror

In September of 2001, the same year the Buddhas were destroyed, the Twin Tower attacks took place in New York and the world's focus was firmly reorientated towards Afghanistan and the Middle East. By October that year, the United States began its occupation of Afghanistan, with allies such as Britain and Australia following closely behind, in a campaign codenamed "Operation Enduring Freedom." Just like the justification for every conflict that had come before, this war too was shrouded in public rhetoric of liberation, this time embedded in democratic principles and ideological salvation. By 2004, the first democratically elected government was installed, which, though heralded as a good news story and

a win for the occupying forces, in reality, did little to assuage the harsh realities of life in a conflict zone for many Afghan people.

If the rest of the world changed drastically with 9/11, the situation in Afghanistan remained much the same. The year the United States and allies entered the country was the twenty-fifth consecutive year of conflict since the Saur Revolution. There were generations who had known nothing but the insecurity of war. Conservative estimates suggest that Operation Enduring Freedom, which would indeed "endure" for years to come, led to the deaths of hundreds of thousands of Afghan civilians through direct and indirect causes. There is, in fact, no official count of how many Afghan people have been killed as a result of the war on terror.

The other lasting legacy of the war is that it brought squarely into mainstream consciousness a dominant narrative of division, based on the idea of enmity and irreconcilability between East and West. This neatly segmented people on a global scale to either "us" or "them," based on racial and religious identity, with the norms set by Western dominance. Its corrosive simplicity, and its implicit demands for conformity, would come to undermine global cohesion in escalated, sometimes unforeseen, ways. Times had changed and precious little, including conflict, would remain localized. We were all living in a world that was more interconnected than ever before, yet with dangerous and fabricated clashing ideologies—the differences between them being conflated and used to justify further atrocities. The world was at a tipping point.

Reversing the paths traveled: voyagers return to Afghanistan

It was against such a global backdrop that, in April 2012, my sisters, nieces, brother-in-law, and I returned to Afghanistan. We crossed the border on foot, from Pakistan into Afghanistan at the Khyber Pass. We were retracing our footsteps in the opposite direction to that taken 27 years earlier, when, as children, our parents had bundled us together and, under a cloud of uncertainty and blind hope, negotiated our way out of Afghanistan and into our future. We were returning as adults, pulled forward by an allure we were yet to understand—perhaps, simply, by a need to know more.

The most striking thing about Afghanistan was its epic landscape, lush and fertile on our arrival in spring. The giant silhouettes of the snow-capped mountains of the Hindu Kush, and the cascading layers of crumpled and velvety peaks that lay staggered beneath them, inspired an overwhelming reverence, extracting an almost involuntary relinquishment of ego. The peaks played with light and shadow throughout the day, creating a natural rolling spectacle from daybreak to dark, always with an ethereal luminosity. At the base of the peaks, vast valleys of bright green grass and crops stretched out like gently rolling oceans. It was a landscape with its own distinct energy that easily contextualized the vulnerability of being human, and which had watched history unfurl.

One of the most immediate and unexpected aspects of Afghanistan that lingers as an enduring memory, was the invitation it extended to us. It wrapped us in a warm embrace, as if it had been permanently imprinted with the memory of seeing us come into the world. Many things seemed strangely familiar—from the worn, but still kind, features of its people, to the social mannerisms, to the sweet smell of the spring air.

We spent the first few days in Kabul, where we were met by the family of my brother-in-law, Sayed Ayaz Ashna. Sayed himself was an expert cook, trained by a long line of men in his family who held their own secrets of Afghan cooking. His father, in particular, was renowned for the pickles, preserves, and jams he could so skilfully make, using native seasonal vegetables and fruits such as quince. We sampled these extensively, usually alongside our rustic and communally prepared meals.

Then we made our way from Kabul towards Jalalabad—one of our final stops in the country before we had departed as refugees, decades earlier. We stayed in the nearby district of Dari Noor—"valley of light"—in the family home of my mother's cousin. It was a place where my mother and her siblings had spent their summers as children, alongside their extended family. We were welcomed into his home as though we were his own children. Youngsters from the extended family peeked shyly and inquisitively at us from behind walls, their little faces beautifully olive with bright green eyes, framed by tousled golden hair. They were testament to the marbled global heritage that courses through Afghan veins.

Dari Noor is a self-sufficient and breathtaking valley, with clear brooks, nestled between endless green hills and surrounded by fruit orchards, banana plantations, and wildflowers. The mountains sit in the distance behind—presenting an exquisite horizon. We spent the nights sleeping under an inky sky, the stars hanging low and blotchy. Our meals were made with ingredients from the valley. There were soft cheeses, called paneer, paired with large, purple-tinged raisins; sweet and almost perfumed honey; sabzi, or wild spinach, cooked with native onions and chili; chai, made using pure mountain water pumped from a well; and long breads, made with local grains. There was an organic, unadulterated, and rustic taste to everything. Food was served in beautiful blue-green Istalif pottery, made in the Afghan mountain villages, using unique and ancient glazing techniques. We were extended the type of hospitality that Afghanistan is famed for—deeply encoded in the region's genetic memory, but which felt even more poignant given it was unfolding during times of hardship, when people had very little but still insisted, by their honor, upon giving their guests the best they had to offer.

Afghanistan was, in a word, disarming, mainly perhaps for its long list of paradoxes. Kabul was a city pockmarked by decades of conflict, with crumbling buildings and poor infrastructure, overcrowded with people crammed into small living quarters. But, driving through the streets, one also saw extreme wealth—gated communities, expensive mansions, and shiny SUVs. It was obvious that, for all the poverty, there were riches to be made for those opportunistic enough to benefit from war. Tanks rolled through the streets while children played nearby, their peals of laughter ringing through the air. There was the loud roar of military helicopters overhead, while the soft melodious bells of the ice-cream man, peddling his cart of shir yakh, tinkled on the street. There was art, gardens, creeping bougainvillea, and beautiful splashes of color decorating otherwise beige and morose buildings. Parents feared that every day their children went to school could be their last—victims of some random blast—and yet the children dutifully made their way to lessons each day. There was a tendency for war to break; but with so much broken all around, those who still lived did so with a deep appreciation for what remained. There were reasons everywhere for despondence and misery, yet the people we encountered showed endless kindness and concern for our wellbeing and comfort, as their guests or simply as travelers passing through the land.

But if for us, as voyagers into the nation, there was room to feel enthralled by the experience of reconnecting with our ancestral lands, there was also a deep awareness of the difficulties of life in a region which, for almost four decades, had been assaulted by the ploys for control of various regimes.

All had presented themselves with different ideologies, sometimes worlds apart, but with those differences always somehow denominating to the same acts of depravity and authoritarianism. Time and again, it would prove that the most important thing about each party vying for control was not the content of their ideology, but that they had dogmatically subscribed to an ideology in the first place—one which they were arrogantly intent on imposing upon the Afghan people.

In the country's recent history alone, the communist regime, the mujahideen, the Taliban, and the United States and its allies had each entered Afghanistan in order to mold it into its own image, using the carrot of

into, and the paradoxes which defined it, all of which refused to be squeezed into the simple binaries and narratives of disconnection that dominated the world we were living in.

Kutchi Deli Parwana—the gypsy

We returned from Afghanistan with a deeper understanding of how our worlds and cultures fit together. We had learned that time and place had a big influence on what could be created. If those inside Afghanistan were still making objects of beauty and preserving their heritage in creative ways while bombs and blasts exploded overhead, then oceans away in Australia, almost three decades since we

Sayed Ayaz Ashna, at Kutchi Deli Parwana

propaganda and the stick of outright violence for its own material or ideological gains. This encroachment upon the spirit of the people who, as an unlikely amalgam of cultures and worlds, were perhaps never designed to be uniform, but free to live and adapt on their own terms, was always destined for incoherence and ruin. How the Afghan people had carried on through such sustained force, managing to hold on to and offer something of their own that was deeper and kinder and could not be extinguished, was testament to the existence of a powerful counterforce to human depravity—of a true and selfless will to life. The momentum of living was great.

We left Afghanistan with more of ourselves fallen into place. We had connected more dots—about ourselves, our parents, our ancestors, the land we had been born

had left Afghanistan, we could also contribute to the human story of our times through creativity and food—but it would be expressed and have significance in different ways.

In 2014, two years after visiting Afghanistan, we opened the next chapter in our family's culinary story—a second food spot, named Kutchi Deli Parwana. This was an amalgamation of our worlds and the experiences that shaped us. Kutchi is Farsi for "nomad" or "gypsy." The word was apt. It encapsulated our journeying from Afghanistan to Australia, but also our internal roaming and our desire to stay settled and connected only with the depths of ourselves that mattered—with the parts of the human spirit that could not be extinguished by outside forces.

The small lunchtime space reflected the sights we had absorbed on our travels through Afghanistan. There we had seen the bright pops of color, splashed through small food spots, decorated with a mix of fluorescent and incandescent light, and tiled with decorative geometric patterns. We had seen the street vendors offering piping hot naans cooked over hotplates, fried parcels of vegetables dipped in batter with herb chutneys poured on top, and deliciously tangy bowls of a vinegared chickpea dish called shor nakhot—all without compromising on taste. We had gained more insight into the ways that food was so closely intertwined with art and all aspects of beauty in Afghan culture, and so we hand-painted the walls of our little shop with scenes from old Persian miniatures. And, importantly, we had learned more about how food is inseparable from a deep sense of generosity, invitation, gratitude, and honoring one another, with little space left for pretence.

The evolving nature of culture

As we offered these things at Kutchi Deli Parwana, we did so in recognition that they were significant because of the setting in which our life story had unfolded. Living in Australia, the idea of offering something quickly in line with the pace of contemporary life, but still deeply connected to old ways of cooking, in a setting that placed an emphasis on the arts in a way revered in ancient and contemporary Afghanistan, resonated as a way to further bridge between our worlds. Importantly, we had also recognized that we were part of a reality in which social norms were increasingly being defined by the perception of an irreconcilability of East and West, and this perception was having devastating real-world outcomes. Kutchi Deli Parwana was not necessarily a way of rebutting the invalidity of this fiction, but of bypassing it, and offering something of ourselves instead. We ourselves were testament to the historic amalgamation of ways that infused civilization—a narrative that had long been silenced— and, in honoring this, we were driven to create in ways unbound by the deceit of disconnection so many norms in our world were increasingly coming to reflect.

We were learning something, too, about how creative cycles of culture unfold, fettered to and shaped by the iterations of the human story immediately preceding it. If, for my great-grandmother, during times of peace and nation-building, food was about owning the identity that had emerged alongside the global concept of the nation state, for my grandmother food became about preserving and sharing this. By the time my mother reached adulthood she was living in a time of conflict and food became a way to stay connected to what was being supressed and at risk of being lost. By the time we grew up, on lands far from our original home, and in deeply fractured times, our food was about memories of the past. But, increasingly, this remembering was significant because it invalidated the many fictions of our present, while attempting to offer a narrative reflecting on our inextricable links— the echoes of a shared existence.

Alongside these evolutions, there were also things that stayed constant. Food was always about connection to, and sharing with, one another and the times we had each generationally found ourselves in. Food was transcendent—it held fast beyond the breakdowns and suffering that were part of the human make-up, and which had kept each generation bound to the last in a chain of interlinked expressions.

The recipes in this chapter illustrate the further bridging of the many influences in our lives, particularly driven by the experience of returning to Afghanistan for the first time since leaving as small children. The street-food influence, a time-honored part of Afghan cuisine, and whose concepts we thought important to share through Kutchi Deli Parwana, is captured in this chapter's recipes, alongside the pickles and preserves so lovingly prepared by family we encountered on our travels. These recipes bring us back, full circle, in the cycle of creativity that fuels culture to respond to the challenges of the day, while sourcing its legitimacy and value by staying rooted in its own past—if only to contribute in meaningful ways to our increasingly shared future.

SHOR NAKHOT

شور نخود

Shor nakhot is a tangy, vinegary chickpea snack that is traditionally sold by street-food vendors in Afghanistan, mainly in Kabul. The protein-packed chickpeas serve as a quick pick-me-up between meals. Served in a special vinegar dressing, shor nakhot is made to order as mild or as spicy as you can handle.

This recipe requires some preparation. The dried chickpeas must be soaked overnight, and then refrigerated overnight once they are cooked, before they can be served in the vinegar dressing.

2 cups (14 oz/400 g) dried chickpeas
1 cup (250 ml) white vinegar
2 teaspoons ground red pepper, plus extra to serve
1 handful fresh cilantro stalks and leaves, finely chopped
2 garlic cloves, thinly sliced
2 medium waxy potatoes
Salt

Two days before you intend to make shor nakhot, put the chickpeas into a large bowl, cover with at least 2 in (5 cm) water, and leave to soak for at least 8 hours.

Drain the chickpeas in a colander, discarding the water, rinse in cold water, and drain again. Add the chickpeas to a large pot with 5¼ cups (1.25 liters) water, bring to a boil, then reduce the heat to medium and simmer for 50 minutes, or until the chickpeas are cooked through and soft, but still retain their shape. Transfer the chickpeas and water to an airtight container and refrigerate overnight.

The next day, bring the vinegar and 1 cup (250 ml) water to a boil in a small saucepan. Add the ground red pepper, cilantro, garlic, and 2 teaspoons salt, bring to a boil again, and cook for 3–4 minutes. Remove the pan from the heat and set aside for 1–2 hours, until completely cooled.

Meanwhile, in a medium pot, boil the potatoes with the skin on for about 15 minutes, or until tender but not very soft. Once boiled and slightly cooled, peel and thinly slice into discs.

Drain the chickpeas and place in a large serving bowl with the potatoes. Add the vinegar dressing, mix to combine, and serve in small bowls.

PEKOWRAH

1¼ cups (4 oz/120 g) chickpea flour
  (besan)
2½ tablespoons all-purpose flour
Heaped 1 tablespoon cornstarch
1 teaspoon baking powder
1 teaspoon ground coriander
1 teaspoon freshly ground black pepper
1½ teaspoons powdered yellow food
  coloring (available from Indian
  grocery shops)
1 cup (250 ml) chilled water
Sunflower oil, for deep-frying
2 large all-purpose potatoes, peeled and
  very thinly sliced
Chutney sabz (see page 86) and/or chutney
  morcheh sorkh (see page 87), to serve
Salt

These deep-fried vegetable fritters are a typical street food in Afghanistan, made by vendors who set up their large karayee pans for deep-frying on street corners. They can be made using an assortment of vegetables, such as leeks, potatoes, chilies, or onions, and are best enjoyed with a chutney to dip into.

This recipe uses only potatoes and is a favorite of my brother-in-law Sayed who, growing up in Afghanistan and Pakistan, would snack on these savory bites on his way home from school.

Whisk the dry ingredients and 2 teaspoons salt in a bowl to combine. Still whisking, slowly add the water, to create a smooth, runny, lump-free batter.

In a medium pot or deep-fryer, heat enough oil for deep-frying to 350°F (180°C) on an oil thermometer.

Dip the potato slices into the batter to fully coat, then gently and carefully lower them into the hot oil using tongs. Fry the pekowrahs in batches without overcrowding the pan, and turning once, for 3–4 minutes each side, or until they are golden and crisp. Serve immediately with homemade chutney.

SAMBOSA

سمبوسه

2 small boiling potatoes, such as
    red or Yukon gold, diced
1 small carrot, diced
1 yellow onion, very finely diced
1 teaspoon cumin seeds
1 teaspoon ground ginger

FOR THE DOUGH
2½ cups (10½ oz/300 g) all-purpose flour
1 teaspoon baking powder
4 tablespoons sunflower oil, plus extra
    for deep-frying
½ cup (125 ml) warm water
Salt and freshly ground black pepper

Sambosas are stuffed, deep-fried pastries, popular in Afghanistan and across the subcontinent. When my parents lived in Kabul, Indian street-food vendors (who had been in Afghanistan for many generations since Mughal rule) were renowned for making the best sambosas. They are usually served with chutney sabz (see page 86), chutney morcheh sorkh (see page 87), or jaan-e-ama yogurt dip (see page 191).

◆

Bring the potato, carrot, and ½ cup (125 ml) water to a boil in a small saucepan. Reduce the heat to medium and simmer for 15 minutes, or until all the water has been absorbed and the vegetables are soft and cooked through. Transfer the vegetables to a large mixing bowl, add the onion, and mix to combine well. Add the spices, 2 teaspoons salt, and 1 teaspoon freshly ground black pepper, and mix gently to combine. Set the filling aside while you make the dough.

Whisk the flour, baking powder, and 1 teaspoon salt in a bowl to combine. Add the oil and mix to combine with your hands. Make a well in the center, add the water to the well, and combine with your hands to form a dough. Knead for about 5 minutes, or until the dough is smooth and firm; if it's a little sticky, add a spoonful of flour and knead a little more to ensure the dough is firm. Cover the bowl with a tea towel and set aside at room temperature for 20 minutes to rest.

Once rested, divide the dough in half. Lightly dust a work surface with flour, then evenly roll out one half to make a 12 in (30 cm) circle. Use a 4 in (10 cm) cookie cutter to cut out as many rounds as you can; you should get about nine. Place a heaped 1 tablespoon of cooled filling into the center of each circle and lightly moisten around the edge with water. Fold over one side of the circle to meet the other and press to seal the edges together to make semicircles. Gently imprint decorative lines into the sealed edges of some of the sambosas with a fork. For a decorative rope-patterned edge, pinch, twist, and press to seal the dough all the way along edge. Roll out the remaining dough to make a 12 in (30 cm) square, then cut into nine 4 in (10 cm) squares. Place a heaped 1 tablespoon of the filling in the middle of each square, bring the opposite corners together, and press the edges to seal and form a triangle.

When you have about 18 sambosas ready to fry, fill a heavy-based saucepan one-third full with oil and heat to 350°F (180°C) on an oil thermometer. Fry the sambosas in small batches, turning once, for 2–3 minutes each side, or until they are golden brown and little bubbles appear on the surface of the pastries. Remove with a slotted spoon and drain on paper towels to absorb excess oil. Serve the sambosas hot.

FALOODA

فالوده

4¼ cups (1 liter) cold whole milk
Vanilla ice cream, to serve
Coarsely crushed pistachios and
   rose petals, to garnish

FOR THE MAGHOOT JELLO
1 teaspoon yellow food coloring
4 tablespoons cornstarch

FOR THE ROSE SYRUP
Generous 1 cup (8 oz/225 g) sugar
1 tablespoon rosewater
2 teaspoons pink food coloring

FOR THE BASIL SEEDS
2½ tablespoons dried basil seeds
   (sabja; available from Asian
   grocery shops)
2½ cups (625 ml) boiling water

This milky rosewater-infused cold dessert is popular in the subcontinent. It is served in a tall glass, with layers of rose syrup, pieces of maghoot jello, ice cream, milk, and nuts. In Afghanistan, falooda is sold in small, colorfully decorated ice-cream shops known as shir yakh feroshees.

This recipe has several different components—rose syrup, soaked basil seeds, and maghoot jello—which are all made separately and assembled together to make falooda.

◆

To make the maghoot jello, bring 2 cups (500 ml) water and the food coloring to a boil in a saucepan. Stir the cornstarch with 2½ tablespoons cold water in a small bowl to form a smooth paste, then add 2½ tablespoons of the colored boiling water and mix to make a slurry. Slowly add the tempered cornstarch to the boiling water, stirring continuously to prevent lumps from forming. As soon as the mixture begins to boil again after 2–3 minutes, pour it into a large shallow heatproof dish, and refrigerate to set and cool for at least 2–3 hours. Cut the maghoot jello into small cubes by cutting it into thin strips horizontally and then vertically, and set aside.

To make the syrup, add the sugar and 1 cup (250 ml) water to a small saucepan over high heat, stirring to dissolve the sugar. Bring to a boil, and boil without stirring for 2–3 minutes, or until the syrup thickens and reaches 233°F (112°C) on a candy thermometer. Stir in the rosewater and pink food coloring to combine well and set aside to cool.

To prepare the basil seeds, place them in a bowl and pour the boiling water on top. Set aside to soak for about 15 minutes, or until the seeds are sticky and gelatinous. Set aside to cool.

To assemble the falooda you will need 6 tall glasses. Put 2½ tablespoons of the rose syrup into each glass. Add a heaped 1 tablespoon of diced maghoot jello, followed by a heaped 1 tablespoon of soaked basil seeds. Next, pour in cold milk to three-quarters full, add a scoop of vanilla ice cream, and garnish with crushed pistachios and rose petals.

Serve immediately, with a straw and a spoon.

SHIR CHAI

2½ tablespoons loose-leaf black tea
Generous 1 cup (8 oz/225 g) sugar
6 cardamom pods, bruised
4¼ cups (1 liter) whole milk

This Afghan sweet milk tea is usually enjoyed at breakfast time, alongside hot fresh naan bread and sweet preserves, or in the late afternoon.

With its delicate spiced aroma, it has become a favorite at our Kutchi Deli Parwana, where it's served either hot or iced.

Place 1½ cups (375 ml) water in a medium saucepan with the tea, sugar, and cardamom over high heat and stir until the sugar dissolves. Bring to a boil, then reduce the heat to medium, and simmer for 5 minutes to let the tea steep and the flavors combine.

Add the milk to the pan and increase the heat. Bring to a boil once again, then reduce the heat to medium, and simmer for 15 minutes, so the flavors fuse completely.

Strain through a fine sieve into a bowl, discarding the tea leaves and cardamom pods. Pour the shir chai into a teapot and enjoy while hot, or leave to cool and serve chilled.

MAASHAWAH

Maashawah is a thick, hearty soup packed with protein-rich legumes and mini koftas. Because it includes several ingredients that were not always so readily available in Afghanistan as they are today, it was traditionally made as a treat when family and close friends were gathered together.

This soup became a favorite with my sisters and I for its rich and layered flavors, and it is also a winter favorite at Kutchi Deli Parwana. It's served with a cooling yogurt sauce, which is delicious but entirely optional. Start the recipe a day ahead to soak the chickpeas and beans.

◆

Cover the chickpeas and kidney beans with at least 2 in (5 cm) cold water in a bowl and set aside for at least 8 hours. They will expand as they soak up the water, so you will need a bowl large enough to accommodate this.

Drain the chickpeas and beans in a colander, rinse, and drain again. Add them to a medium pot, cover with at least 2 in (5 cm) fresh water, and bring to a boil, then reduce the heat to medium and cover with a lid. Simmer for 35 minutes, or until the chickpeas and beans are soft, but still retain their shape. Drain in a colander, discarding the water, and set the chickpeas and beans aside.

Put the mung beans and pearl barley into a separate pot and cover with at least 2 in (5 cm) water. Bring to a boil, then reduce the heat and simmer for 20 minutes, or until they are soft. Set aside without draining—the green color and flavor released into the water by the mung beans give this recipe its name.

½ cup (3½ oz/100 g) dried chickpeas
½ cup (3½ oz/100 g) dried red kidney beans
½ cup (4 oz/113 g) mung beans
½ cup (3½ oz/100 g) pearl barley
½ cup (125 ml) sunflower oil
1 garlic clove, finely chopped
1 medium yellow onion, finely diced
2 large tomatoes, finely diced
Heaped 1 tablespoon tomato paste
2 teaspoons ground turmeric
1 medium carrot, peeled and finely diced
5¼ oz (150 g) green beans, trimmed and cut into small pieces
1 quantity mini koftas (see page 116; optional)
Dried mint, to serve
Salt

FOR THE YOGURT SAUCE
½ cup (4½ oz/130 g) plain yogurt
½ teaspoon garlic powder

Heat the oil in a large pot over high heat and sauté the garlic for 1 minute, or until fragrant. Add the onion and fry for 3–4 minutes, or until golden brown. Stir in the tomatoes and tomato paste, and cook for 2–3 minutes, then stir in the turmeric and 1 tablespoon salt (or to taste). Pour in 6 cups (1.5 liters) water and bring to a boil. Add the carrot, beans, chickpeas, red kidney beans, pearl barley, and mung beans, including the cooking liquid, and boil for 8–10 minutes, or until the vegetables are tender and the soup has slightly reduced and thickened.

For the yogurt sauce, whisk together the yogurt, garlic powder, and ½ teaspoon salt in a small bowl.

Maashawah can be served at this point, drizzled with the yogurt sauce, if using, and scattered with dried mint. Otherwise, prepare the mini koftas and add to the soup just before serving, garnished with dried mint and the yogurt sauce, if you like.

AUSH

Aush is a traditional thick soup including various seasonal vegetables and hand-rolled, knife-cut noodles, revealing the Chinese and Mongolian influences on Afghan cuisine. The noodles take time to prepare and, like maashawah soup (see page 223), aush was a dish made occasionally and communally with family and friends.

Have your lamb kofta sauce (see page 46) or vegetarian tomato sauce (see page 47) ready before you start making aush.

To make the noodles, whisk the flour and 1 teaspoon salt in a bowl to combine. Add the oil and use your hands to combine, then add the warm water little by little, mixing by hand just until a firm dough forms—you may not need all the water. Knead the dough on a work surface lightly dusted with flour for 5 minutes, or until smooth and elastic. Return the dough to the bowl, cover with a tea towel, and set aside at room temperature to rest for 15 minutes.

Dust the work surface generously with flour and roll the dough to a paper-thin circle 12–16 in (30–40 cm) in diameter; this is important, since it forms the length of the noodles. Lightly dust with flour and gently roll up into a firm but not too tight log. Using a sharp knife, cut the log at ½ in (1 cm) intervals, then unfurl the coils into long noodles, as shown in the photo over the page. Sprinkle generously with flour to prevent them sticking together and set aside until needed.

To make the yogurt dressing, whisk the yogurt, garlic, and ¼ teaspoon salt until smooth, and refrigerate until you're ready to serve the soup.

½ cup (125 ml) sunflower oil
2 medium yellow onions, finely diced
2 garlic cloves, crushed
1 moderately hot fresh red chili, finely diced
2 teaspoons ground turmeric
4 large tomatoes, finely diced
1 small turnip, peeled and finely diced
1 small carrot, peeled and finely diced
¼ cauliflower, finely chopped
½ quantity lamb kofta sauce (see page 46) or vegetarian tomato sauce (see page 47), to serve
Dried mint, ground red pepper, and finely chopped green chili, to garnish
Salt

FOR THE NOODLES
1¾ cups (8 oz/225 g) all-purpose flour
2 teaspoons sunflower oil
½ cup (125 ml) warm water

FOR THE YOGURT DRESSING
¼ cup (2½ oz/70 g) plain yogurt
¼ teaspoon garlic powder

Heat the oil in a large pot over high heat. Add the onions, garlic, and fresh red chili, reduce the heat to medium, and sauté for 5 minutes, or until the onions are golden brown. Add the turmeric and 2½ tablespoons salt, stir to combine, and fry for another minute. Stir in the tomatoes and cook for 5–10 minutes, or until they break down and a thickened sauce forms. Add 12 cups (3 liters) water, increase the heat to high, and bring to a boil. Add the turnip, carrot, and cauliflower, and boil for about 10 minutes, or until the vegetables are starting to become tender. Add the noodles to the pot and boil for 6–8 minutes, or until they're al dente. By this time, the vegetables should also be tender and the soup slightly thickened.

Ladle the aush into serving bowls, including a mix of soup, noodles, and vegetables in each bowl. Add a spoonful or two of lamb kofta or vegetarian sauce to taste, drizzle with yogurt sauce, and garnish with dried mint, ground red pepper, and green chili to taste. Enjoy while hot.

Making noodles for Aush (page 224)

SHORWA

شوربا

4 tablespoons sunflower oil
1 large yellow onion, diced
1 garlic clove, finely chopped
1 lb 9 oz (700 g) lamb shoulder, bone in,
  cut into medium-sized chunks
2 large tomatoes, diced
3 dried bay leaves
Heaped 1 tablespoon garam masala
Heaped 1 tablespoon ground red pepper
Heaped 1 tablespoon coriander seeds,
  crushed
2 large boiling potatoes, such as Yukon
  gold or red, peeled and quartered
1 carrot, peeled and cut into
  large chunks
Small handful fresh cilantro leaves, to
  serve
Salt

Shorwa is a thin, translucent soup filled with meat and vegetables, making it an ideal lunchtime staple in Afghanistan, due to the protein and nutrients it provides. Traditionally, shorwa is eaten with torn pieces of naan bread dropped into it to soak up the flavors of the broth.

This shorwa is made using a pressure cooker for deliciously tender meat and vegetables.

Add the oil to the pan of a pressure cooker over high heat and fry the onion and garlic for 5 minutes, or until softened and golden brown. Add the lamb and fry for 4–5 minutes, or until the meat is seared. Stir in the tomatoes, bay leaves, spices, and 1 tablespoon salt and cook for 2 minutes, to combine flavors. Add 7 cups (1.75 liters) water to the pan and safely secure the lid.

Bring to high pressure, then reduce the heat to medium and cook for 20 minutes. Carefully reduce the pressure and remove the lid. Add the potatoes and carrot, and reseal the lid. Increase the heat to high, bring back to high pressure, and keep it there for 2–3 minutes.

Carefully release the pressure, remove the lid, and ladle the shorwa into individual bowls. Scatter with cilantro leaves and serve.

KAROO

1 cup (250 ml) sunflower oil,
  plus 1 tablespoon extra
1 large yellow onion, finely diced
3 garlic cloves, finely chopped
Heaped 1 tablespoon finely grated fresh
  ginger
2 moderately hot fresh red chilies,
  finely chopped
4 large tomatoes, finely diced
3 teaspoons brown mustard seeds
2 teaspoons ground turmeric
2 teaspoons cumin seeds
1 teaspoon fenugreek seeds, coarsely
  crushed with a mortar and pestle
1 teaspoon ground red pepper
1 teaspoon garam masala
1 teaspoon chaar masalah (see page 21)
⅔ cup (2 oz/60 g) chickpea flour (besan)
4 cups (2¼ lb/1 kg) plain yogurt
1 cup (250 ml) boiling water
Handful of fresh curry leaves, to serve

Karoo is a thick soup that highlights the flavors of caramelized onion and yogurt. Traditionally in Afghanistan, this was peasant food made in the provinces. As children, it became one of our favorite soups, because of the delicious and balanced flavors, which we'd enjoy with thick pieces of naan bread.

◆

Heat 1 cup (250 ml) of the oil in a pot over high heat and fry the onion, garlic, ginger, and chilies for 5 minutes, or until the onion is soft and golden. Add the tomatoes and stir occasionally for 3–4 minutes, or until they start to break down. Stir in 2 teaspoons of the mustard seeds (setting the rest aside), along with the other spices and 1 tablespoon salt (or to taste). Mix to combine and cook for 2–3 minutes, or until fragrant.

Meanwhile, whisk the chickpea flour and yogurt in a bowl until a smooth paste forms. Add this mixture to the pot with the boiling water, stirring continuously to ensure the yogurt doesn't split, for 4–5 minutes, or until the mixture comes to a boil. The karoo should thicken to the consistency of a creamy soup. If it's still a little runny, keep reducing it over high heat. If it's too thick, add a little more water.

Before serving, fry the remaining teaspoon of mustard seeds and the fresh curry leaves in a small saucepan with the extra tablespoon of oil over high heat for 2–3 minutes, or until they start to crackle.

Serve the karoo in individual bowls, garnished with the fried mustard seeds and curry leaves.

TORSHI BEMASALAH

نرشی بمسالہ

10 cups (2.5 liters) white vinegar
4 beets, each trimmed and cut into
  8 wedges
Heaped 1 tablespoon fenugreek seeds
2½ tablespoons white sugar
2½ tablespoons ground red pepper
3½ oz (100 g) cauliflower, separated into
  florets, larger florets cut in half
2 carrots, peeled, trimmed, and thickly
  sliced diagonally
2 turnips, each trimmed and cut
  into 8 wedges
2 red banana peppers, thickly sliced
  diagonally
2 Persian or Lebanese cucumbers, trimmed
  and halved lengthways
2 baby eggplants, trimmed and halved
  lengthways
Salt

Torshi means pickles, and there are several recipes that are easily adaptable for personal tastes and seasonal produce. This torshi recipe is bemasalah, which means it's prepared without many spices or oil, as opposed to the torshi masalahdar (see opposite), which includes plenty.

As we traveled in Afghanistan, my brother-in-law Sayed's family expertly prepared various pickles, which we enjoyed as an accompaniment to most main meals. In particular, torshi is traditionally always eaten alongside sholeh goshti (see page 121).

Making torshi was a way for us to preserve seasonal produce. They are usually made in large batches in late fall so families can continue to enjoy seasonal vegetables such as turnip and pumpkin over the following months. To prevent any mold developing, torshi are traditionally stored in large clay pots, with care taken to ensure that no water or contaminated utensils comes into contact with them.

Put the vinegar, beets, fenugreek, sugar, ground red pepper, 6 cups (1.5 liters) water, and 2½ tablespoons salt in a large pot.

Bring to a boil, then add the cauliflower, carrots, turnips, and peppers, bring to a boil again, and boil for 15 minutes, or until the carrots have softened slightly. Add the cucumbers and eggplants and boil for 3 minutes, or until they just begin to soften and absorb the vinegar.

Remove the pan from the heat, gently transfer the vegetables to a large bowl using a large slotted spoon, and set aside to cool. Reserve the vinegar mixture in the pot and set aside separately to cool.

Pour the cooled vinegar mixture over the vegetables and mix gently to combine so that the vegetables do not break. Refrigerate torshi in a large covered sterilized jar overnight before eating. If the pickles are kept cool and dry, and the jars are well sterilized, torshi bemasalah should keep for 3–4 weeks. Enjoy alongside any main meal.

TORSHI MASALAHDAR

This recipe for torshi, or pickles, is slightly tangier than torshi bemasalah (see opposite) due to the inclusion of citrus. It is made using an assortment of seasonal vegetables, but with less vinegar and more oil and spices for a sharp, sour taste.

◆

Bring the vinegar, 4¼ cups (1 liter) water, and 2½ tablespoons salt to a boil in a large pot. Add the cauliflower, carrots, turnips, lemons, cucumbers, garlic, and eggplants, and bring to a boil again. Boil for 4–5 minutes, or until the carrots and turnips are slightly softened, then remove the pan from the heat. Transfer the vegetables to a large dry bowl using a large slotted spoon, discarding the liquid, and set aside for 2 hours to cool completely.

Add all the spices, dried chilies, and 1 tablespoon salt to the cooled vegetables, stirring gently to coat and combine. Cover the bowl with a lid and set aside for 3 hours for the flavors to infuse. Pour the oil and extra vinegar over the vegetables and mix gently to combine well. Refrigerate torshi masalahdar in a large covered sterilized jar for at least 1 week before enjoying as an accompaniment to any main meal.

4¼ cups (1 liter) white vinegar, plus ⅓ cup (80 ml) extra
3½ oz (100 g) cauliflower, separated into small florets
2 carrots, peeled, trimmed, sliced lengthways, and cut in half
2 medium turnips, trimmed and cut into ¾ in (2 cm) cubes
2 small lemons, unpeeled, cut into ¾ in (2 cm) pieces
2 Persian or Lebanese cucumbers, trimmed and cut into ¾ in (2 cm) cubes
8 garlic cloves, cut in half
2 baby eggplants, trimmed and cut in half lengthways
Heaped 1 tablespoon fennel seeds, coarsely crushed with a mortar and pestle
Heaped 1 tablespoon coriander seeds, coarsely crushed with a mortar and pestle
Heaped 1 tablespoon nigella seeds
Heaped 1 tablespoon mustard seeds, coarsely crushed with a mortar and pestle
Heaped 1 tablespoon cumin seeds, coarsely crushed with a mortar and pestle
Heaped 1 tablespoon fenugreek seeds
Heaped 1 tablespoon ground turmeric
Heaped 1 tablespoon ground red pepper
8 whole dried long red chilies
2 cups (500 ml) olive oil or mustard oil (mustard oil will give you a more intense flavor)
Salt

From left to right:
Torshi bemasalah (page 232);
Torshi masalahdar (page 233)

MORABAYEH SEB

مربای سیب

2 teaspoons cooking caramel
  (available from supermarkets or
  Asian grocery shops)
1 lb 2 oz (500 g) golden delicious or
  fuji apples, left whole and peeled
7 cups (3 lb/1.3 kg) sugar
1 teaspoon ground cardamom
Peel of 1 lemon, juice of ½

Morabayeh seb is an apple preserve, where whole apples are stewed in syrup with a hint of citrus.

When my mother was growing up, she loved to make jams, and her father would proudly show off the large glass jars full of those that she'd made. In Afghanistan, preserves and jams such as this are enjoyed with hot naan bread and fresh butter for breakfast, or as a sweet bite after a meal.

Bring 6 cups (1.5 liters) water and the cooking caramel to a boil in a large pot, then add the apples. Boil for about 15 minutes, or until the apples are soft, but still hold their shape. Remove the apples from the liquid and set aside.

Measure the liquid to check you still have 6 cups (1.5 liters); if not, top it up with more water. Return the liquid to the pot and place over high heat. Add the sugar and bring to a boil, without stirring, until the syrup reaches 233°F (112°C) on a candy thermometer.

Stir in the cardamom, lemon peel, and juice to combine. Add the apples, bring to a boil, and reduce the heat to medium. Gently simmer the apples in the syrup for 15–20 minutes, or until they appear translucent. Remove the pot from the heat and set aside to cool.

Transfer the apples and syrup, including the lemon peel, to large sterilized jars, cover, and refrigerate. Morabayeh seb will keep for up to a month.

MORABAYEH BEHEE

مرباءِ بهی

In Afghanistan, quince grows in abundance, and is a favored fruit from which to make jams and preserves. This recipe for preserved quince uses citrus to balance the sweetness, and beets for their brilliant pigmentation, which deepens the color. Enjoy it with naan bread for breakfast, or simply as a sweet treat.

1 lb 2 oz (500 g) quince, each peeled, cored, and cut into 8 wedges
2 beets, trimmed and quartered
7 cups (3 lb/1.3 kg) sugar
1 teaspoon ground cardamom
Peel of 1 lemon, juice of ½

Bring 6 cups (1.5 liters) water, the quince, and beets to a boil in a large pot and boil for 15 minutes, or until the quince is tender, but still holds its shape. Gently remove the quince and beets from the liquid, discard the beets, and set the quince aside in a bowl.

Measure the liquid in the pot to ensure you still have 6 cups (1.5 liters); if not, top it up with more water. Return the liquid to the pot over high heat. Add the sugar and bring to a boil, without stirring, until the syrup reaches 233°F (112°C) on a candy thermometer. Stir in the cardamom, lemon peel, and juice to combine. Add the quince, bring to a boil, then reduce the heat to medium and simmer for 15–20 minutes, or until the quince becomes translucent.

Transfer the quince and syrup, including the lemon peel, to sterilized jars, cover, and refrigerate. Morabayeh behee will keep for up to a month.

MORABAYEH ANJIR

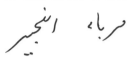

1 lb 12 oz (800 g) dried figs
1 tablespoon cooking caramel
  (available from supermarkets
  and Asian grocery shops)
5¼ cups (2¼ lb/1 kg) sugar
2 teaspoons ground cardamom

This whole fig jam, using dried figs, was one of my maternal grandfather's favorite things to prepare. He would make large pots of it to share with family and friends. Part of the fun was the preparation. When my mother and her siblings were children, they would wait impatiently for their father to finish making the jam so they could lick the pot clean. Before he had barely extracted the last fig, they would race for the pot. By the time they'd each had a turn, the pot would be clean.

When my siblings and I were children growing up in Australia, my mother would prepare this jam in memory of her father. Inevitably, the same battle for licking the pot clean would ensue.

It's the interlinked expression of traditional food that has connected us through the generations.

Bring 8½ cups (2 liters) water, the figs, and cooking caramel to a boil in a large pot, and boil for 20 minutes, or until they soften. Remove the figs from the liquid using a slotted spoon and set aside in a bowl.

Add another 8½ cups (2 liters) water to the pot and bring to a boil. Add the sugar and cardamom to the pot and stir to dissolve the sugar. Bring to a boil again and boil without stirring for 20 minutes, or until the syrup reaches 200°F (100°C) on a candy thermometer.

Add the figs to the syrup and boil for 20 minutes, or until the figs absorb the color and flavor of the syrup and the syrup thickens further.

Transfer the figs and syrup to sterilized jars, seal, and refrigerate. Morabayeh anjir will keep for up to a month.

AFTER US

فصل ششم

The untold stories of tomorrow

Trying to determine the future in which the realities of Afghanistan will unfold remains a vexing pursuit. With the country still plagued by ideological differences, and the violent imposition of will by local and foreign forces, it is something that remains clouded in uncertainty. But one thing that is becoming more apparent is the degree to which existing dogmatic narratives of control are proving less relevant, yet increasingly threatening, to our collective future.

The dominant narratives that have prevailed have created norms that have driven the world to its present position at the cusp of crisis. From the maritime revolutions to the earliest imperial conquests, which justified the exploitation of people and resources in the name of nation-building and glory, these histories normalized a vision of power based on the suffering of others. Alongside the military revolutions and technological evolutions that took place, the potency of the power behind occupations and the redirection of people's will also magnified. The systems that came to prevail were those that not only sanctioned, but valued, the extraction of the world's resources, with no thought to sustainability, and the ego-driven oppression of people based on divisions such as color, gender, ethnicity, language, or creed. Regions like Afghanistan have long endured the brunt of this depraved definition of power. But, increasingly, we are all living out the various consequences of a world in which we exist in exile from our deeper nature, where the scale of questions we can ask, and the depth of self we can draw upon, has been expertly narrowed to create sanitized and sanctioned versions of reality.

The clash defining our times is now between reality and the narratives that have long tried to contain it. Issues such as climate and biodiversity breakdowns, the spread of conflict and disease, or the mass displacement of people, cut effortlessly across the fabricated boundaries of fear and nationalism that have been constructed around us. As challenges spread and grow in their immensity, the narratives that helped bring them into existence are being exposed as irrational, dangerous, and antithetical to the survival of our species. And, as these existing narratives disintegrate, we are being beckoned forth, challenged to unmask deeper realities and to transfigure into the next version of ourselves.

The globally interconnected nature of these consequences betrays a critical and long-buried truth that needs to be revived once more: our histories, and our fate as a species, are deeply intertwined. Afghanistan, sitting at the heart of the ancient Silk Road—a network of routes which, incidentally, are becoming increasingly relevant once again—is a symbol of the interconnectedness and mutual dependence that has guided the course of the evolution of civilization. Beyond the lens of fear and hostility that has become the dominant association with Afghanistan today, what is far more prescient in times such as ours is to probe beyond the constructed schisms and to glean from its story the capacity for human civilization to cooperate and cross-pollinate.

In today's world, driven by exponential advances in technology, we are more interconnected than ever before, with people, goods, ideas, and conflict moving at speeds and in proximities that are unprecedented. Along with the challenges this brings, it also carries the potential for many boons—the chance to listen to, and build upon, every ancient wisdom we have collected as a civilization and can now readily and easily share. The call of our times is to find the narratives that fit—the ones that reflect our potential for shared and boundless horizons. Our future perhaps depends most on our ability to find a collective answer.

This ability, in turn, depends on our capacity to reorient away from the confining narratives of disconnection that have limited our collective human potential, and to metamorphose into a version of ourselves that acknowledges the degree to which we are, each and everyone, vestiges of the natural universe. Realizing that we are all part of the same whole does not mean subsuming our unique or culturally defined identities into oblivion—rather the opposite. It means acknowledging them, but in a far deeper way than that which presently resounds, unseduced by the exclusionary labels of identity that categorize people according to hierarchies of perceived worth, and driven instead by the ability to see the transcendent connections between things— to recognize that the rivers of self empty into the oceans of all, which lap against the shores of the universe.

This interconnection, as a necessity for survival and evolution, is a central tenet of the significance of food and Parwana to my family. To this day, Afghan cuisine bears the hallmarks of the various cultures, from the Mediterranean through to the Far East and beyond, which met on ancient lands and fused together ingredients, philosophies, and traditions to create something at once old and new. By recognizing this story, we are able to see food as more than just sustenance. It is an ever-evolving narrative that captures the sentiments and the stories of a generation, who will pass it on to the next to build upon, and to make their own in light of their own realities, before passing it on again. It is the story of our earth, its cycles and geography, mixed in with this shared evolution of human civilization. It is an edible and non-verbal bypassing of the narratives of disconnection and otherness. All of this is further underpinned by a culture of sharing meals with an unwavering devotion to hospitality, arising from a belief in the sacredness of others and in the universality of our collective human experience.

By staying close to the untainted and uncontained narrative engrained in food, we have been offered a means to look back while looking forward, to see ourselves as individual and universal, to open doors by closing others, to be steeped simultaneously in joy and suffering. In essence, we have an opportunity to work towards experiencing and affirming life through the process of reconciling these seeming dualities.

What this reconciliation means, if anything, for tomorrow, we cannot know. All that any of us can offer in earnest is more energy and more stories to weave together into the fabric of our collective future. The story shared here, in these pages, is but one strand in the web of existence in which we are each a part. With deeper consciousness of the extent to which we are all bound together, we will, perhaps, be best positioned to create the untold stories of the tomorrows still to come.

Acknowledgments

I would like to acknowledge my entire family, who were generous in their participation and their recollection of stories and emotions that have been woven together to form the narratives in this book. Further acknowledgment to my father, Zelmai Ayubi, whose Farsi handwriting is scattered throughout these pages. Thanks also to Corinne Roberts, as well as Justin Wolfers, Madeleine Kane, James Brown, and the whole publishing team. And finally, deep gratitude goes to family members and other icons of Afghanistan who have long passed, and whose memories have been conjured in the book.

About the Author

Durkhanai Ayubi is involved with the day-to-day responsibilities of the Ayubi family's eating places in Adelaide, Australia—Parwana and Kutchi Deli Parwana. She also writes freelance opinion-editorial pieces for a range of newspapers and websites, and is an Atlantic Fellow of the Atlantic Institute, which is based at the Rhodes Trust in Oxford, England.

Index

A

Achaemenid Empire 15
Afghan cuisine, origins of 18–19
Afghan hospitality 19, 166, 207
Afghanistan, history and historic
   figures of
      19th century 58
      20th century 100–109
      1964 constitution 101
      Afshar, Nader Shah 59
      Amin, Hafizullah 104, 105–106
      Anglo–Afghan wars 60–61
      Buddhism, spread of 15
      communism, rise of 104–105
      displacement of citizens 108–109,
         162–163, 167
      Durrani, Ahmad Shah 59–60
      Ghaznavid Dynasty 16
      Ghurid Dynasty 16
      Great Game, the 60–61, 162
      Greek influence 15
      Hekmatyar, Gulbuddin 107, 165
      Hotak Empire 59
      independence from Britain 61–62
      Khan, Amanullah 61, 62, 63
      Khan, Daoud 101, 102, 104
      Khan, Dost Mohammad 60
      Khyber, Mir Akbar 103–104
      Kushan Empire 15–16
      Mongol Empire 16–17
      Mughal Dynasty 18
      mujahideen resistance 107, 204
      Nadir Shah 63
      Paleolithic Age 14
      Russia, 19th-century rise of 60
      Safavid Empire 17
      Saffarid Dynasty 16
      Sassanian Empire 16
      Saur Revolution 104
      September 11, 2001, ramifications
         of 206
      Silk Road 14, 16, 60, 245
      Soviet occupation 105–106
      Soviet withdrawal 164–165

      Taliban, emergence and rise of
         204–206
      Taraki, Noor Mohammad 104
      Timurid Empire 16–17
      United States occupation 206
      Zahir Shah 63, 101, 164–165
Afshar, Nader Shah 59
agriculture 15
Aï Khanum 15
Alexander the Great 15
almonds
   Afghan milk fudge 152
   almond cookies 156
   "seven fruits" 22
Amin, Hafizullah 104, 105–106
apples
   preserved apples 236
apricots, dried
   "seven fruits" 22
art 15–16
Ashna, Sayed Ayaz 207
Ayubi family *see also* individual
   family members
      ancestry 61–63, 105
      Australian resettlement 165–167
      Kutchi Deli Parwana
         establishment 208–209
      leaving Afghanistan in 1985
         108–109, 162–163
      return to Afghanistan in 2012
         206–208
Ayubi, Durkhanai (author) 106
Ayubi, Farida 9, 102, 104, 108–109, 166
Ayubi, Fatema 102
Ayubi, Raihanah 166
Ayubi, Zahra 106
Ayubi, Zelaikhah 105
Ayubi, Zelmai 102, 106, 108–109,
   165–166, 166

B

Babur 17–18
Balkh 15, 16
Bamiyan 206

barley
   mung bean soup 223
basil seeds
   falooda 217
beans, green
   green bean curry 172
beef
   beef patty kebabs 81
   meatball curry with rice 122
   shaami kebab 131
   sticky rice with mung beans 116
beets
   pickled vegetables 232
   preserved quince 239
Begram 14
braises *see* curries, braises & stews
breads
   flatbread, stuffed 48–55
   naan bread with extra oil 83
   naan flatbread 82
   sweet bread 132
Buddhas of Bamiyan 206

C

cabbage
   dumplings, steamed 38–41
cardamom
   Afghan milk fudge 152
   clotted-cream chai 136
   cream rolls 149
   "elephant ears" 142
   fried cardamom cookies 145
   milk custard 141
   milk tea 218
   preserved apples 236
   preserved quince 239
   rose and pistachio ice cream 196
   sweet bread 132
   whole fig jam 240
carrots
   mung bean soup 223
   pickled vegetables 232
   rice with carrots and raisins 113
   spiced pickled vegetables 233

thick soup with noodles 224
thin soup with vegetables 228
cauliflower
  cauliflower curry 175
  pickled vegetables 232
  spiced pickled vegetables 233
  thick soup with noodles 224
chaar masalah 21
chai
  shir chai 218
  clotted-cream chair 136
chana dal
  lamb kofta sauce 46
  tomato sauce, vegetarian 47
chicken
  chicken curry 184
  chicken flatbread stuffing 53
  chicken kebab 73
  rice with chicken 129
  turmeric and yogurt-braised
    chicken 74
chickpea flour
  thick yogurt soup 229
  vegetable fritters 213
chickpeas
  chickpea curry 180
  mung bean soup 223
  vinegared chickpeas 210
chilies
  red chili chutney 87
  spiced pickled vegetables 233
China
  Han Dynasty 16
  Silk Road, significance for 13–14
chutneys
  green chutney 86
  red chili chutney 87
cilantro
  green chutney 86
compotes
  "seven fruits" 22
cookies
  almond cookies 156
  cookies for Nowroz 29
  "elephant ears" 142
  fried cardamom cookies 145
  salted Afghan cookies 155
  sweet cookies for Eid 146
  walnut cookies 157
cranberries
  rice with chicken 129
cream rolls 149

cucumbers
  Afghan-style salad 84
  pickled vegetables 232
  savory yogurt drink 195
  spiced pickled vegetables 233
  yogurt and cucumber dip 191
curries, braises & stews
  braised eggplant with yogurt
    dressing 169
  braised pumpkin with yogurt
    dressing 179
  cauliflower curry 175
  chicken curry 184
  chicken kebab 73
  chickpea curry 180
  green bean curry 172
  kidney bean curry 186
  lamb curry 183
  lamb kebab 69
  lentil curry 170
  meatball curry with rice 122
  mixed mushroom curry 187
  okra curry 173
  pan-cooked lamb kebab 78
  potato curry 176
  spinach and lamb curry 25
  turmeric and yogurt-braised
    chicken 74
  turnip and lamb curry with rice 130
  yogurt-braised lamb 77
custard, milk 141

D
dahl 170
desserts see sweets
dips
  smoked eggplant dip 190
  yogurt and cucumber dip 191
displacement 108–109, 162–163, 167
dogh 195
drinks
  clotted-cream chai 136
  milk tea 218
  rose syrup 140
  savory yogurt drink 195
dumplings
  boiled chive dumplings 44–45
  steamed dumplings 38–41
Durrani, Ahmad Shah 59

E
eggplants
  braised eggplant with yogurt
    dressing 169
  pickled vegetables 232
  smoked eggplant dip 190
  spiced pickled vegetables 233
eggs, Afghan breakfast 65
"elephant ears" 142

F
falooda 217
figs
  whole fig jam 240
fish, crispy fried 30
flatbread, stuffed 48
  chicken flatbread stuffing 53
  chive flatbread stuffing 52
  potato flatbread stuffing 52
  pumpkin flatbread stuffing 53
flour halwah 91
food, origins of Afghan 18–19
food, cultural and familial significance
    166, 204, 208–209, 246
"four spices" 21
fritters, vegetable 213
fruit, dried see specific dried fruits
fudge, Afghan milk 152

G
garlic
  spiced pickled vegetables 233
garlic chives
  boiled chive dumplings 44–45
  chive flatbread stuffing 52
Genghis Khan 16
Ghafour, Bibi Hamida 62, 62–63
Ghafour Khan, Abdul 62
Ghaznavid Dynasty 16
Ghurid Dynasty 16
ginger and walnut ice cream 199
green beans
  green bean curry 172
  mung bean soup 223

H
Hafizullah, Amin 104
Hamida 62–63
Han Dynasty 16
Hekmatyar, Gulbuddin 107
Herat 16–17
Hotak Empire 59

I

ice cream
    ginger and walnut ice cream 199
    rose and pistachio ice cream 196
indigenous peoples of Afghanistan
    14–15
Iraq as cradle of civilization 13

J

jam see also preserves
    whole fig jam 240
Jelabi 33–34

K

Kabul 60
kebab
    chapli kebab 81
    shaami kebab 131
kebabs (skewers) see skewers
kebabs (braises and other meat dishes)
    see curries, braises & stews
Khan, Abdul Ghafour 62–63
Khan, Amanullah 61, 62, 63
Khan, Amin 102
Khan, Daoud 101, 102, 103, 104
Khan, Dost Mohammad 60, 61
Khan, Emir Sher Ali 61
Khyber, Mir Akbar 103–104
kidney beans
    kidney bean curry 186
    mung bean soup 223
kofta
    lamb kofta sauce 46
    meatball curry with rice 122
Kushan Empire 14, 15
Kutchi Deli Parwana, origins of 208–209

L

lamb
    lamb curry 183
    lamb kebab 69
    lamb kofta sauce 46
    lamb skewers 66
    meatball curry with rice 122
    pan-cooked lamb kebab 78
    rice with carrots and raisins 113
    shaami kebab 131
    spinach and lamb curry 25
    sticky rice with lamb 121
    sticky rice with mung beans 116
    thin soup with vegetables 228
    turnip and lamb curry with rice 130

yogurt-braised lamb 77
lentil curry 170
lettuce
    Afghan-style salad 84

M

maghoot 137
Majrooh, Bahaouddin 107–108, 163–165
Majrooh, Shamsuddin 62, 101
mantu 38–41
Mariam, Bibi 102
Mauryan Empire 15
milk
    Afghan milk fudge 152
    falooda 217
    ginger and walnut ice cream 199
    milk custard 141
    milk tea 218
    rose and pistachio ice cream 196
    sweet cookies for Eid 146
mint
    green chutney 86
Mongol Empire 16–17
Mughal Dynasty 18
mung beans
    mung bean rice 125
    mung bean soup 223
    sticky rice from Ghorband 120
    sticky rice with lamb 121
    sticky rice with mung beans 116
mushrooms
    mixed mushroom curry 187

N

naan
    naan bread with extra oil 83
    naan flatbread 82
Nadir Shah 63
noodles
    noodle rice 126
    thick soup with noodles 224
Nowroz 15, 19
nuts see specific nuts

O

okra curry 173
orange rind rice 114

P

Pachah Sahib, Azrat Shah 61–62
Pakistan 162–163
Parwana restaurant

origins 9, 167
    ramifications 204, 246
pastries
    cream rolls 149
    "elephant ears" 142
    stuffed fried pastries 214
peppers
    pickled vegetables 232
    red chili chutney 87
pickles
    pickled vegetables 232
    spiced pickled vegetables 233
pistachios
    Afghan milk fudge 152
    rose and pistachio ice cream 196
    "seven fruits" 22
potatoes
    lamb curry 183
    potato curry 176
    potato flatbread stuffing 52
    stuffed fried pastries 214
    thin soup with vegetables 228
    vegetable fritters 213
    vinegared chickpeas 210
preserves see also jam
    preserved apples 236
    preserved quince 239
pumpkin
    braised pumpkin with yogurt
    dressing 179
    pumpkin flatbread stuffing 53
    pumpkin halwah 95

Q

quince
    preserved quince 239

R

radishes
    Afghan-style salad 84
raisins
    mung bean rice 125
    rice with carrots and raisins 113
    "seven fruits" 22
red kidney beans
    kidney bean curry 186
    mung bean soup 223
rice
    culinary significance of 110
    Kabuli palaw 113
    meatball curry with rice 122
    mung bean rice 125

noodle rice 126
orange rind rice 114
plain white rice 111
rice with carrots and raisins 113
rice with chicken 129
sticky rice from Ghorband 120
sticky rice with lamb 121
sticky rice with mung beans 116
Roman Empire 13, 16
rosewater
Afghan milk fudge 152
Afghan-style jello 137
falooda 217
rose and pistachio ice cream 196
rose syrup 140
Rumi (poet) 16

S
Safavid Empire 17
Saffarid Dynasty 16
saffron
jelabi 33–34
rice with chicken 129
semolina halwah 90
salad, Afghan-style 84
Salehi, Nouria 165–166
Sassanian Empire 16
Saur Revolution 104
semolina halwah 90
"seven fruits" 22
shaami kebab 131
Silk Road 14, 16, 60, 245
skewers, lamb 66
soup
mung bean soup 223
thick soup with noodles 224
thick yogurt soup 229
thin soup with vegetables 228
Soviet occupation of Afghanistan
105–106
spiced pickled vegetables 233
spices
chaar masalah 21
"four spices" 21
spinach and lamb curry 25
stews see curries, braises & stews
Sufism 61
sweets see also cookies
Afghan milk fudge 152
Afghan-style jello 137
cream rolls 149
"elephant ears" 142

flour halwah 91
fried cardamom cookies 145
jelabi 33–34
preserved apples 236
preserved quince 239
pumpkin halwah 95
semolina halwah 90
"seven fruits" 22
whole fig jam 240

T
Taliban, emergence and rise of
204–206
Taraki, Noor Mohammad 104
tea
clotted-Cream chai 136
milk tea 218
Timurid Empire 16–17
tomatoes
Afghan breakfast eggs 65
Afghan-style salad 84
braised eggplant with yogurt
dressing 169
cauliflower curry 175
chicken curry 184
green bean curry 172
kidney bean curry 186
lamb curry 183
lamb kofta sauce 46
meatball curry with rice 122
pan-cooked lamb kebab 78
potato curry 176
sticky rice from Ghorband 120
sticky rice with lamb 121
sticky rice with mung beans 116
thick soup with noodles 224
thick yogurt soup 229
tomato sauce, vegetarian 47
turnips
pickled vegetables 232
spiced pickled vegetables 233
thick soup with noodles 224
turnip and lamb curry with rice 130

V
vegetable fritters 213

W
walnuts
ginger and walnut ice cream 199
"seven fruits" 22
walnut cookies 157

women in Afghanistan 63, 100, 101,
163, 205

Y
yellow split peas
chicken curry 184
lamb kebab 69
turmeric and yogurt- braised
chicken 74
yogurt-braised lamb 77
yogurt
braised eggplant with yogurt
dressing 169
braised pumpkin with yogurt
dressing 179
green bean curry 172
homemade yogurt 26
kidney bean curry 186
lamb curry 183
mung bean soup 223
pan-cooked lamb kebab 78
potato curry 176
savory yogurt drink 195
sticky rice with mung beans 116
thick soup with noodles 224
thick yogurt soup 229
turmeric and yogurt- braised
chicken 74
yogurt and cucumber dip 191
yogurt-braised lamb 77

Z
Zahir Shah 58, 63, 101, 164–165
Zoroastrianism 15

Published in 2021 by

INTERLINK BOOKS
An imprint of Interlink Publishing Group, Inc.
46 Crosby Street
Northampton, Massachusetts 01060
www.interlinkbooks.com

Publisher: Corinne Roberts
American edition publisher: Michel Moushabeck
Editorial manager: Justin Wolfers
Design manager: Madeleine Kane
Cover design: Madeleine Kane
Design concept: James Brown, U.F.O. Agencies
Editor: Alison Cowan
American edition editor: Leyla Moushabeck
Recipe editor: Krishna Mathrubutham
Narrative editor: Jane Price
Photographer: Alicia Taylor
Stylist: Deborah Kaloper
Recipes: Farida Ayubi
Food assistant: Fatema Ayubi
Production Director: Lou Playfair

Library of Congress Cataloging-in-Publication Data available
ISBN 978-1-62371-875-6

Color reproduction by Splitting Image Color Studio Pty Ltd, Clayton, Victoria
Printed by C & C Offset Printing Co. Ltd., China

To request our complete 48-page, full-color catalog, please call us toll-free at
1-800-238-LINK, visit our website at www.interlinkbooks.com, or e-mail: sales@interlinkbooks.com.